THE
HAPHAZARD
YEARS

The Haphazard Years

HOW AMERICA HAS GONE TO WAR

by

GEORGE C. REINHARDT

&

WILLIAM R. KINTNER

Doubleday & Company, Inc.
Garden City, New York
1960

Library of Congress Catalog Card Number 60–13744
Copyright © 1960 by George C. Reinhardt & William R. Kintner
All Rights Reserved
Printed in the United States of America
First Edition

FOREWORD

IN THE FALL OF 1957 THE SOVIET UNION CATAPULTED THE FIRST earth satellite into the skies. All over the world, the launching of the Russian Sputnik was regarded as a challenge to American technological supremacy and, more importantly, to our national security. The American reaction to this dramatic Soviet scientific achievement revealed a widespread awareness that twentieth-century military security had become inescapably dependent upon technological progress.

Fear that we might be falling behind the Soviet Union in technology led to sweeping inquiries into the U.S. educational system. It precipitated widespread, if unproductive, discussion of the role of science and scientists in American society. It evoked a series of plans for reorganizing the Department of Defense. This concern seems altogether natural today even though over the last several decades there has been little or no recognition of the interplay between technology and American military policy.

But recognizing the influence of technology on military policy does little to clarify what this influence has been or, ideally, ought to have been. To better understand this crucial interplay, the Social Science Research Council awarded a grant to the authors in 1955 to study the influence of technology on

7

American military policy from the Spanish-American War until the outbreak of World War II in 1939. Our studies undertaken with this grant comprise the first five chapters of this book. In concluding this work we have felt impelled to extend our viewpoint, without detailed analysis, through the familiar events of the Second World War and the dozen years of the Nuclear Age that have followed.

The past half century of American military experience coincided with a period which opened up more technological advances than mankind had achieved in all previous time. The application of this constantly accelerating technology to warfare brought new and vast problems. Yet during the centuries' long record of military clashes marking the birth and death of nations, as many decisive victories were achieved by tactical innovation as were won by technically superior weapons. Time and again, the so-called civilized powers have been defeated by so-called backward, primitive peoples. As late as World War II, startling changes in tactics and organization decided major campaigns even though jet aircraft, German V-weapons, and the atomic bomb were in the arsenals of the contenders.

Within the military profession, as in others, the capacity of men's minds to cope with such a flood of technological change has been severely strained. Military policy in America and many other countries has sometimes failed to anticipate potentially superior weapons. It has been notoriously slow in adjusting organization and tactics to them. So, too, many nations, our own especially, have only belatedly appreciated the impact of new superweapons upon traditional diplomacy and international relations.

As we look into an uncertain future, the impact of tomorrow's technology looms large indeed. The technical tasks of readying America to face that future are enormous. Our leaders must decide to put weapons into quantity production often when those weapons are still in blueprint stages. They must, in addition, create an industrial complex and a military organization geared at every point to the weapons they select. To them falls also the responsibility of forecasting what new weapons of attack and defense our potential foes will develop. Being democratic leaders they must do all this without detriment to the freedom which is the American way of life. Yet this aim need not, and probably cannot, be so tender with the American standard of living, which currently connotes luxuriant affluence.

We propose to concentrate upon one essential aspect of these complex problems, one which ultimately depends upon the decisions of the American people themselves, not merely those of scientists, statesmen, and generals. The ability of the United States to establish sound security policies requires a thorough public understanding of the relationships between technology and all other elements that comprise military power. American military policy, no less than our technology, has been and will continue to be shaped by the will of the American people. A critical examination of the many facets of technology's influence upon military policy in our recent history will contribute to such an understanding. Only an enlightened public can ensure that past mistakes are not repeated, that our earlier achievements are improved upon.

Consequently this book seeks to discover from official archives and many other historical sources some light out of the past to illuminate the search for American security in tomorrow's world, a world where battles may be fought with weapons unimaginable to us today.

The authors gratefully acknowledge advice and assistance in the preparation of this study. Mention has been made of the grant in aid by the Social Science Research Council which supported the considerable task of reviewing source materials and preparation of the original manuscript. Both authors have benefitted from their professional association with research organizations primarily engaged in relating current and projected technology to military strategy, i.e., the Rand Corporation and the Operations Research Office of Johns Hopkins University respectively. At the Rand Corporation, James F. Digby and Wallace H. Hastings generously devoted their time to critical review, offering many helpful suggestions. Also at Rand, John C. Hogan's efforts to guide the manuscript to its publisher proved invaluable.

The deft editorial skill of Walter F. Hahn, executive editor of *Orbis*, the quarterly published by the University of Pennsylvania's Foreign Policy Research Institute made this study far more readable. The publication of much of Chapter VII in *Orbis*, January 1959, provided encouragement. Both Rand and the Foreign Policy Research Institute have provided administrative assistance to the writing of this book. While recording our gratitude for this assistance the views expressed here as well as responsibility for factual accuracy of statements made belong entirely to the authors.

WILLIAM R. KINTNER   GEORGE C. REINHARDT
Washington, D.C.   Santa Monica, California

April 1, 1960

CONTENTS

CHAPTER I

A TEMPORARY AWAKENING

THE ROLE OF AMERICA'S INDUSTRIAL TECHNOLOGY IN shaping our national military policy or, more relevant, the interaction of the two, has been the subject of much fruitless investigation. Inquiries usually centered around our entry into wars that most of us, officials as well as public, could not or would not foresee. Invariably during and after the wars in our history, various government agencies have elaborately investigated scandals or military reverses in a frenzied search for scapegoats. These fact-finding (but not always disclosing) forays produced few positive results. Whatever lessons emerged were dimmed by emotion and political controversy. Rarely have these lessons been intelligently assimilated into the public consciousness or conscience.

Argument so heated seldom sheds much light. Energy is dissipated in side-stepping or assigning blame. Lessons are either ignored or quickly forgotten. Even the dedicated Brigadier General Emory Upton, in his post-Civil War examination of American military policy,[1] devoted more

[1] Emory Upton, *The Military Policy of the United States*, Government Printing Office, Washington, D.C., 1917.

15

time to belaboring legislative shortcomings than to constructive proposals. Congress, Continental or Federal, the invariable whipping boy in our democracy, has in fact never failed to provide what "the people" really wanted.

Unemotional research, as objective as data permits, should replace the brickbats of the past. Our real concern is less with convicting long-dead "criminals" or pillorying departed incompetents than with fathoming the significance of our techno-military history. What are the reasons that caused civilian and soldier to be so often at loggerheads . . . or were they, really?

Our Army, largest and senior service in our national military establishment is, and has ever been, the servant of the state—meaning in this country, an instrument of the popular will. As such the Army's technological lead, or lag, with respect to civilian technological progress needs to be studied in sound perspective but not without a saving grace of humor, for even humor can be found in a generally grim story. A parallel analysis of the Navy will be easier though scarcely as simple as twentieth-century trends imply. Prior to the Civil War and again for several decades late in the nineteenth century, technical obsolescence, the price of national indifference, branded our naval establishment deceptively as the agent of a scientifically backward nation.

Criticism of U. S. Military Policy

Offhand criticism of U.S. military policy for its apparent negligence could be likened to carping at a champion athlete's style—insisting he should have won by a wider margin. America's technology was always harnessed primarily to the pursuits of peace. Hindsight tells us that a more generous and imaginative proportion of that technology's fruits given to our military would have saved lives and dollars in the successive conflicts which have periodically engulfed our nation. Indeed, more judicious policies could probably have prevented some of those wars from occurring. Yet a study of the influence of U.S. military policy upon history might show that even though our technological development has overwhelmingly stressed peace our present wealth and position of world power are largely due to participation in wars.

Who can prove by quantitative measurements, by "controls" in the scientific manner, that diversion of technological effort to military ends would have made this country, as we know it today, a better home for its millions of inhabitants? Would we have been wiser in our possession of ready military strength than we proved in its lack? Might the diverted technologies have grown into a crushing martial juggernaut? Secure in the American tradition one might ignore so fantastic a risk: yet, who can say to what extent a greater emphasis on military preparedness might have retarded our unparalleled social advances? Would we, in that case, have fought more wars or fewer? Changing the fundamental culture (way of life if you prefer) of a large population sets in motion vast forces whose vectors and strength are unforeseeable.

Genesis of Study

In undertaking this search into those oft-discussed, never really heeded, lessons of the interaction of civil-military technologies in our national past, the quest is for facts and their interpretation, not fault finding. The genesis of such a study naturally lies in the formative years of our nation. The United States of America, encountering the Industrial Revolution in its extreme youth, grew to world power at a startling rate under that impetus.

True, we had formidable allies in this rise: a plethora of natural resources, the beneficial shield of geographical isolation from interfering neighbors and a favorable climate. Yet the key to our success has been the spirit in which we brought these assets to bear in the mastery of technological processes. This national "dynamism" which, perhaps fortuitously, never seriously outpaced our ability and readiness to deal with the social problems that followed inevitably in its wake, has usually been absent in our military efforts. Save for brief periods of emergency, our treatment of national defense has been as parsimonious and indifferent as our devotion to industrial prowess has been unstinting. Yet, paradoxically, all our wars hastened rather than slowed the surge of national growth and individual prosperity.

Our national dynamism, had it been harnessed to warlike goals, might have fashioned a mid-twentieth-century *Pax Americana*, surpassing that of ancient Rome. As it was, the expansion of the original thirteen colonies into a nation that spanned the North American continent was the product of pragmatic growth rather than of conscious planning. Equally paradoxical, this country achieved its victories, prior to 1940 certainly, by sheer strength and awkwardness, ignoring rather than utilizing the very technologies which based its power and usually furnished the remote though fundamental causes for our military involvement.

American devotion to peace, heightened in the twentieth century, does not adequately explain this paradox. Any impartial investigation can quickly rule out cowardice or greed as primary causes. The inconsistency between our unexcelled technological development in the skills of peace (manpower has always been the most costly way of doing work in the United States) and our laggard allocation of those skills to our national defense remains an unsolved mystery.

Traditional Antipathy for Militarism

Traditional American antipathy for anything savoring of "militarism," or perhaps fundamentally of discipline, took root naturally enough in a nation formed by dissenters from Europe's intolerant monarchies and religions. But in three hundred years, as colonies and nation, we have fought too often and too determinedly to perpetuate unrealistic attitudes toward military matters: nevertheless American irrationality on this subject appears to have increased with time. During the past seventy years a technologically preeminent United States has repeatedly sent its armed forces into combat less effectively equipped than their foes.

The technological lag in our generally successful ventures into warfare might be partially explained by General Fuller's assertion that "the loser learns most from a war."[2] On the other hand our twentieth-century victories deny Holley's comment: "wars are governed . . . by such fractions of [technological] development as have been recognized and incorporated into military doctrine."[3]

[2] J. F. C. Fuller, *Armament and History*, Scribner's, 1954, p. 142.

[3] I. B. Holley, Jr., *Ideas and Weapons*, Yale University Press, 1953, p. 18.

Complaisance bred of the "we can do it again if we have to" mentality ignores hard fact. Today, we find ourselves and our nation in a period of world tension that is unique in its technological significance, awesome in its sinister potential. Only in this decade has it become possible to destroy whole nations by swift acts of war telescoped into a single night. Never has the courage and devotion of defenders, unsupported by the most highly developed weapons and skills, been so impotent. Even the untapped human and industrial potential of nations sink into insignificance before stark combat power, continuously poised and instantly ready.

Mere survival increasingly relies upon the entire range of military-scientific development—from brilliant ideas to production lines' finished weapons and men proficient in their operation. Today's "absolute" weapon may be the obsolete weapon of tomorrow. A mere decade has sufficed for an exponential growth in bombs' explosive power: from tons of TNT, through kilotons, to megatons. Other factors vital to modern warfare—transportation, communication, fire control—have almost kept pace.

In such a world, reasons for the sinusoidal rise and fall of U.S. military strength, despite our continuous and broad technological advances, cry for analysis and identification. We have long treated our defense establishment as an "expedient of a struggle rather than the permanent source of a nation's safety. If this policy were possible in the past, it is no longer so, and each succeeding year diminishes its probabilities."[4] This warning is more cogent now than when it was voiced fifty years ago by General Homer Lea, a hunch-

[4] Homer Lea, *The Valor of Ignorance*, Harper & Brothers, 1909, p. 217.

back soldier of fortune, who returned to America from foreign wars to warn his countrymen of their danger.

Lea's observations are not invalidated by the essential caution that military force alone as the "permanent source of a nation's safety" can also be as fraught with risk. We may deplore with Lewis Mumford that "war has been perhaps the chief propagator of the machine"[5] though this causal relationship is least applicable to our homeland. We might possibly take fright from General J. F. C. Fuller's assertion that the "dependence of industry upon war has become more vital to our economic system than the dependence of war upon industry."[6] But we would have to ignore our own history if we accept Fuller's contention that "as technology advances militarism advances also."

Whatever our views on, and fears of, ancillary evils we must not shut our eyes to reality. What would be mankind's status today had Nazi Germany or Communist Russia outstripped America in the technological race for the atomic bomb? A small group of scientists, many of them foreign born and educated, had the vision and intellect to spearhead the work that prevented such a disaster. As for the future, for some years at least, our nation's—indeed civilization's—fate depends upon the progress of the Free World's scientific and military technologies. How these technologies have interacted in America's recent past may shed light upon our problems in a tomorrow that already casts its heavy challenge upon us.

[5] Lewis Mumford, *Technics and Civilization*, Harcourt Brace, 1934, p. 86.

[6] J. F. C. Fuller, *Armament and History*, Scribner's, 1954, p. 170.

The Frontier's Impact Upon Policy

A profound change in American economy and interests, noticeable only with the passage of years, was concisely recorded by a single sentence of the Census Report for 1890: "The unsettled area has been so broken into by isolated bodies of settlement that there can hardly be said to be a frontier line." The endless, till then, succession of frontiers had played a major role in shaping America's international relations and economic life in addition to absorbing, if not dominating, so much of our military effort on land and even on the sea.

If the dynamism that marked our first century as a nation were not to be suffocated, henceforth it would of necessity be directed into other channels. Whatever new goals we sought, our treatment of technological and military problems was due for drastic changes. They could no longer be so starkly separated without endangering our security. Yet the ancient tradition of anti-militarism was stronger than ever, albeit less bellicosely expressed. The self-reliant frontiersman's blunt contempt for professional soldiery had gradually eroded. A vastly more prosperous, industrialized community turned to self-righteous and less worthy excuses: "too proud to fight," isolationism, neutrality. The impact of our new pre-eminence in technology upon military policy was not appreciated, much less understood.

In the seventy years since the Census Report of 1890 the United States has fought five major wars: against Spain; pacifying the Philippines; defeating the Kaiser; destroying Hitler and the Japanese military caste; achieving a stalemate in Korea. Lesser military embroilments have been legion, from intervention in the several Caribbean republics to landings in Lebanon. The record of our military technology in those years has ranged from disgraceful to merely less than the promise of its civilian counterpart. Deploring past mistakes accomplishes nothing. Learning from hitherto unheeded experience can reshape the future.

But, to return to 1890 when American industry and technology were overtaking those of Europe's great powers, we had only recently terminated our struggle to subdue a continent. From that moment on we inevitably became more aware of our contacts and our incipient struggles, with distant nations. This awakened interest in the world outside our borders focused early upon the tragedy being enacted near our shores in Cuba. There the long struggle for independence from Spain was reaching a climax of bloodshed and brutality. In such a setting the mixture of American sympathy for the underdog, the imperialistic aims of a vigorous minority and unscrupulous journalism propelled us into our initial involvement in an overseas war. In that conflict we acquired remote territories, which were by no means frontiers, along with all the problems—political, economic, sociological, and military—implicit in such acquisition.

The growth of the United States to world power, almost untrammeled by foreign interference, could have happened only in the nineteenth century. The Industrial Revolution transformed western civilization during those hundred years. An economy of scarcity dependent upon manual labor, animal-drawn transportation, and sailing ships altered rapidly and radically. The new age of steam power lowered barriers to travel and communication. Production from the land and the newly created factories expanded manifold. But problems of distribution, of increasing population pressures and changing social structures plagued Europe as it clumsily abandoned a craftsman-rural economy for the first tastes of industrialized society. The historic riots of the English weavers, their livelihood threatened by power-driven looms; the potato famine in Ireland; the dire poverty of the increasing number of factory workers—these typified upheavals whose adjustments absorbed the energies of Europe.

Equivalent problems were ameliorated in the Western Hemisphere by the presence of the very frontiers that only the progress of the Industrial Revolution enabled us to penetrate so swiftly. The tempo of history favored America. An earlier industrial development might well have tempted Europe to brush aside the Monroe Doctrine and to partition North America as well as Africa. A slower pace would have denied the U.S. the shiploads of emigrants, foreign capital investments, and world markets essential to our phenomenal growth.

Industrial-Military Imbalance

When in April 1898 an inflamed public opinion forced the reluctant President William McKinley into war any comparison of American industry and technology with those of Spain reflected hugely in our favor. Restrict the survey to available combat strength however and America's military establishment, notably our Army was definitely inferior. Conflict with decadent Spain disclosed this imbalance between our techno-industrial and military attainments with a series of shocks. Yet an unbroken succession of easy victories, from Admiral Dewey's May 1, triumph in Manila Bay, to the surrender of Santiago, Cuba, July 17, quickly diverted public attention and scotched apprehension. The postwar report of a Presidential Commission which investigated the conduct of the War Department during the conflict received relatively little notice. Despite the critical testimony and constructive recommendations it contained, neither the government nor the recently exercised public heeded its recommendations.

There had indeed been much to excite the American public in the brief course of the war, April 21 to August 12, 1898, and the two frantic months which followed the mysterious explosion of the battleship *Maine* in Havana harbor on February 15. The entire Atlantic coast shrieked for protection from attacks which were completely beyond the capability of Spain's weak Navy. Disease, with typhoid and dysentery taking the heaviest toll, ravaged the troops in Stateside encampments. Later, in Cuba, yellow fever riddled the fighting ranks. Spoiled beef was allegedly issued to soldiers. Movement of units to cantonments and ports of embarkation proved painfully slow; shipment of supplies and equipment for their use lagged interminably. Vessels bearing regiments to hostile shores had no suitable craft for landing them. Reports of the first engagements raised a hue and cry about obsolete weapons and black powder ammunition for our troops confronted by Spanish mauser rifles and smokeless powder. Yet all these embarrassments which a less inept foe might have turned into disasters did not in the actual course of events prevent, or even delay, American victory on land and sea.

Only the Navy seemed to have profited by U.S. technology. Clearly it had been ready with more powerful warships than its adversaries—though not nearly enough to foolishly picket the coast from Maine to Florida at the demand of a frightened public. Congress had evinced its concern over the traditional first line of defense in 1897 by upping Navy Department construction requests from one battleship to three and tripling the number of destroyers. Of course these and some warships authorized by the earlier Cleveland administration were still unfinished. The sea war was fought with five battleships: the *Massachusetts, Indiana, Iowa, Oregon,* and the obsolescent *Texas* but they were enough. Admiral Dewey's squadron that sank the Spanish fleet in Manila Bay comprised no warship heavier than a cruiser. Admiral Pascual Cervera's squadron, destroyed in the only battleship engagement of the war as it fled from Santiago, Cuba, had no chance against the superior American force.

Yet surprisingly, as the President's Commission and other investigations brought to light, our military technologies, even in the Army, had really been up to date. We merely had not been prepared to use them so suddenly on so large a scale. Government arsenals had for years been manufacturing smokeless powder in test lots while Army Ordnance experts argued as to which variety to adopt.

Quality in Insufficient Quantity

The Krag-Jörgensen .30 caliber magazine rifle surpassed Spanish hand weapons but the total number available barely equipped the Regular Army, let alone the far more numerous Volunteers. For the old, .45 caliber Springfield rifles and for the artillery, there was no smokeless powder, nor could any be made quickly available. These arms, in the hands of Lieutenant Colonel Theodore Roosevelt's "Rough Riders" (1st U. S. Volunteer Cavalry) at San Juan hill, became notorious symbols of alleged War Department inefficiency during the acrimonious dispute over the alleged "rescue" of that regiment by the 10th Cavalry (colored) Regiment of the Regulars.

Secretary of War Russell A. Alger plaintively noted in his annual report the magnitude of the Army's mobilization problems, a situation which was destined to repeat itself in aggravated form within twenty years. While the Navy had doubled its strength during the course of the Spanish War, resorting to the extreme of reviving Civil War monitors for "coastal defense," the Army expanded tenfold in ninety days. Executive Orders called for volunteer enlistments in numbers that completely disregarded the Regular Army's absorption capabilities, available equipment, and facilities. The excess over actual manpower requirements later became apparent when two-thirds of the volunteers completed their term of service without ever leaving the continental United States.

Mistakes of this sort, rather than technical incompetence, caused the Army's deaths from disease to exceed battle deaths by more than seven times[7] (345 killed and died of wounds, 2565 died of disease). Only six years later the "newly civilized" Japanese held disease deaths to one-fifth of those occurring in battle in Manchuria.

Thus the U. S. Army in 1898 was more the victim of national policy than of technological neglect. Its equipment and weapons were comparable to Europe's best; even quantitatively adequate for its thin ranks, but woefully insufficient for a sudden tenfold increase. Maintained to fight Indians and used unfortunately to suppress internal disorders—such as at Coeur d'Alene, Idaho, under President Benjamin Harrison's orders and, for President Grover Cleveland, at the

[7] Report of the Adjutant General, 1898, period May–September incl.

Pullman strike in Chicago in 1894—the Army was not designed to fight a foreign foe, least of all on overseas battlefields. Nor was the country geared to meet, in time, the needs of this greatly expanded army.

In many ways the U. S. Army's technical services scaled a new level of competence immediately following the war with Spain and its Philippine aftermath. Gun for gun and rifle for rifle, American equipment equaled that of more militarily renowned nations. Nearly all of its weapons and ammunition were produced in government arsenals operated by a small group of experienced civil service workers and Ordnance officers of the Army and Navy. There was, however, almost no link between the efforts to produce arms inside the military establishment and the surging industrial world outside. No attention was paid to the problem of emergency production by industry, tooling up for large quantities of military hardware in a hurry.

This dichotomy was widened—as explained in a subsequent chapter—by the necessity of equipping American forces—land, sea, and air—with weapons and equipment provided by our European Allies during the First World War. Had we waited for American guns, airplanes, and ships, the war might well have been lost in Europe before our troops were ready to fight.

Postwar Audit

Our enforced dependence upon foreign sources for munitions in 1917–18 could have been avoided had the lessons of 1898 been learned by the United States. An adequate industrial capacity for the needs of our military establishment could have emerged from the war with Spain and the official investigations it inspired. The effort involved would not have burdened our expanding economy though certainly it would have been much too small to have invigorated it.

Either of two courses of action would have been effective: maintaining the U.S. armed services at a level high enough to stimulate a peacetime munitions industry, or placing modest, though profitable, "educational orders" to insure at least stand-by munitions plants. The former was then an unthinkable policy in America; the latter technique was unknown before World War I.

Consequently the military technological progress inspired by the campaigns in Cuba and the Philippine Islands ground to a halt several years after the "emergency." A handful of diligent specialists, not researchers, toiled on in arsenals and navy yards, scrimping on minimum budgets to supply immediate requirements. Only a slim margin of effort or, still scarcer, funds were left to seek improvements in existing items.

"Weapons systems," a term of recent origin suggesting an integration of military equipment and trained men for a single combat task, was beyond the comprehension, though not the technology, of the world of 1900. Recognition of such military dependence upon technology made its first important impact in Britain after the Russo-Japanese War when the "dreadnought" class[8] of capital ships rendered obsolete every other battleship afloat.

In this country, too, our initial approach to "systems"

[8] Named from the British battleship *Dreadnought*, completed in one year (1906–7), carrying 12-inch guns, no "secondary" (8") batteries, and possessing a speed in excess of 20 knots.

developed in the Navy. Its General Board, founded in 1900, reluctantly followed naval historian Mahan's teaching to think of "the fleet," several classes of warships wedded to a common purpose, rather than "flying squadrons" or individual ships "on station." President Theodore Roosevelt, an ardent disciple of Alfred Thayer Mahan, added no small impetus to this advance. He realized after his experience as Assistant Secretary of the Navy that the United States Navy was fortunate that its first foreign foe in a hundred years had been decadent Spain and not a more formidable opponent.

After the naval victory of Cavite, Admiral Dewey's operations against the Manila batteries encountered interference from a technologically superior German squadron. Only the unequivocal intercession of a British admiral, present with an equally powerful force, prevented serious embarrassment to American arms.[9] Ground forces in the conflict against Spain fought, senselessly handicapped by anachronistic tactical organization although the War Department Staff was cognizant of European "divisions of combined arms" and applied that designation to Army units in Cuba and the Philippines. In fact, however, American "divisions" in those campaigns consisted of grouping of infantry regiments under a general officer, practically unchanged from the tactical organization that prevailed in the Civil War.

Dodge Commission Report

Advance hints of ideas concerning "lead time and industrial mobilization" which would later link military and

[9] Henry Cabot Lodge, *The War with Spain*, Harper & Brothers, pp. 26–27.

techno-industrial activities abound in the eight-volume document submitted to the 56th Congress by President McKinley's investigating commission. Headed by Grenville M. Dodge, a Civil War general of Volunteers who later served as a Republican Congressman from Iowa and established himself as a railroad executive, the twelve-man commission included former Governor Urban Woodbury of Vermont and a distinguished doctor from Ohio along with its military members. These last were drawn from both Volunteers and the Regular Establishment with Brigadier General John M. Wilson, Chief of Engineers, the senior military appointee.

The commission's findings exonerated the bitterly maligned War Secretary, Russell A. Alger, but recorded testimony accused a wide range of officialdom. Charges were often apparently sincere opinions rather than facts. Female witnesses described "unbearable hardships and privations" in cantonments; junior officers described supply and equipment shortages; a general asserted "Congress is chiefly responsible [by its refusal] to reconstruct the Army on modern principles, for the bad administration of the Army and its organization."

The real significance of the Dodge Report lay, however, in its specific recommendations. These were clear guides to remedial action, not mere statements of broad policy. Yet their common sense, amply buttressed by the recent lessons of war, received almost no response from either the executive or the legislative branches of the government. In truth they were accorded little attention even in the newly created War College introduced into the Army under Elihu Root's administration of the War Department. Perhaps that was because the Dodge Report's recommendations dealt with considerations primarily logistic—as are all technological-military interactions except weapons research and training of personnel.

The brevity and simplicity of those recommendations permit a sample quotation: "Maintain on hand at all times a complete supply for at least four months for an Army of 100,000 [of] all items which will not deteriorate by storage or which cannot at once be obtained in the open market; making of heavy guns, mortars, carriages, and projectiles requires plants whose installation is a matter of time. . . ." The commission found the miniature Signal Corps had "become of inestimable value" because of technological progress in combat communications and it recommended "a larger Medical Corps." It noted in passing that many deficiencies in equipment were due to "failure to obtain the necessary appropriation" to complete the Ordnance Department's Rock Island Arsenal, whose buildings, completed but nearly empty of machinery, had been designed to produce it.

Small Gains and Larger Misunderstandings

Nevertheless some direct gains accrued to U.S. military technology in three years of intermittent conflict overseas: the Spanish War, its aftermath in the Philippines, and the "police action" to rescue American civilians besieged by the Boxers in Peking. Of these gains, unquestionably the most far reaching were the great strides in military education and the establishment of the Army General Staff system. Both have been too exhaustively recorded and analyzed to require recounting. Yet it was their combined influence which brought civilian educators to admit in various pedagogical journals and reports after World War II, some forty years later, that military instructional (if not educational) skills had outstripped equivalent U.S. civilian pedagogy.

In a different field, Army achievements in sanitary engineering and the well-known conquest of yellow fever benefitted medical knowledge as a whole. General Leonard Wood's cleanup of Santiago, and later of Havana, whether or not it was possible, as the Army historian William A. Ganoe stated, "only by imposing military discipline"[10] upon civilian populations, contained lessons to sanitary engineers and city authorities of America fifty years ago.

In the larger view, however, neither public nor Congressional understanding of techno-military matters underwent any noticeable improvement from either the stress of war or the obvious lessons to be drawn from the struggle. The depth of the government's incomprehension prior to hostilities is typified by its reaction to emergency. On March 9, 1898, twenty-three days after the battleship *Maine* was blown up and amid popular clamor for war, Congress appropriated $50,000,000 "for the national defense . . . to be expended at the discretion of the President."[11] McKinley, in allocating this money, stuck to the literal wording of the act: work upon coastal fortifications. By taking this stand, the Commander in Chief of the nation's armed forces forbade the War Department from placing orders for equipment badly needed by the Army for obviously impending field operations. Yet the hurriedly voted funds could not possibly achieve in many months any appreciable improvement of the neglected state of our coast defenses.

[10] W. A. Ganoe, *History of the U. S. Army*, Appleton, 1924, p. 398.

[11] Act approved March 9, 1898 (*30 Statutes at Large*, pp. 273–74).

This deficiency was of long standing, dating back to the findings of the Board on Fortifications created by Congress in 1885 and reporting to Secretary of War William C. Endicott the following year. The Board criticized the utter lack of systematic fortification in this country and prepared a thorough plan for mounting more than 2300 heavy guns. By March 1898 only 151 of these had been emplaced. Under the spur of emergency this number was doubled[12] by July, yet it was 85 per cent short of the approved but long-ignored plan.

Hysteria on the Atlantic

Inadequate as these defenses were to protect our extensive coast line from a powerful Navy, military strategists dismissed as absurd the contention that the Spanish fleet might approach our shores, let alone bombard our ports. Nevertheless the same public that had compelled the reluctant President McKinley to declare war and had only at this late date awakened to Congressional neglect of seacoast fortifications now panicked at news of Admiral Cervera's weak squadron sailing west from Spain. Not even the full complement of defense measures sought in vain by the Army during a decade would have calmed the rattled coastal communities.[13] Instead "urgent and pressing demands were made by senators and representatives, and local business interests for the immediate erection of seacoast batteries at numerous

[12] Report of the Chief of Engineers for 1898, p. 196.

[13] Compare the situation in World War II, mounting antiaircraft batteries in U.S. cities after Pearl Harbor; deflation of real estate values on the Pacific coast after one Japanese submarine abortively shelled an oil refinery.

points not contemplated in the general scheme of national defense."[14]

This hysteria which magnified the enemy's feeble seapower to grotesque proportions, seriously hampered the Navy Department's active operations in addition to imposing impossible demands upon the Army. As a result Commodore Winfield S. Schley's Flying Squadron—America's strongest —was tied to anchor in Hampton Roads more than a month, a period sufficient for Admiral Cervera to cross the Atlantic unmolested and take refuge in Santiago harbor.

Simultaneous clamor for offensive operations in Cuba resulted in national directives issued completely at cross purposes. While holding the Navy in leash to timid defensive thinking, the government assigned the Army a series of absurdly rash offensive missions. Encouraged by Lieutenant Colonel J. H. Dorst's exploit in landing 7500 rifles and ammunition for Cuban General Claixto García at Banes on Cuba's north coast, the War Department ordered General William R. Shafter to conduct a reconnaissance in force on Cuba's south coast. On April 30 news of Cervera's departure from the Cape Verde Islands caused the Navy to refuse to detach enough warships to form a protecting convoy. The expedition was deferred.

Confusion in the Gulf

One week later the President directed Major General Nelson A. Miles, Commanding General of the Army, to take 70,000 men and capture Havana. Reluctantly the gen-

[14] Report of the Chief of Engineers for 1898, p. 196.

eral explained[15] to his chief the impossibility of this task: nothing like that number of men or equipment for half as many could be obtained; the enemy had over 100,000 troops in or near the city's defenses.

McKinley quickly suspended the ill-advised order but once more Shafter was directed to embark, this time to the north coast of Cuba. Again the Navy demurred, supported by intelligence that Cervera's squadron had appeared off Martinique on May 11, in excellent position to intercept the troopships.

By May 30 the U. S. Atlantic Fleet had bottled Cervera up in the harbor of Santiago. A new objective was given Shafter: capture Santiago and assist in destroying the Spanish squadron. With all authorities demanding haste but doing little to provide material support, the Army plunged awkwardly into an unprecedented and unplanned task—embarking an expedition to land on a hostile shore. All ships were recalled because of erroneous reports of enemy warships, and the false start kept the troops sweltering in overcrowded transports for five days. Finally, on June 14, 32 jampacked troopships departed carrying almost 17,000 men. Although two months had been consumed in readying this ill-equipped force, totaling less than half the strength of the enemy's troops in Santiago province alone, another 10,000 and most of the artillery was left behind for lack of shipping.

On the other side of the world, Admiral Dewey impatiently awaited Army reinforcements to capture Manila. Except for one small brigade which sailed May 25 the rest of the force, some 11,000 men, which participated in the capture embarked late in June. The tedious 6000-mile voyage

[15] Nelson A. Miles, *Serving the Republic*, Harper & Brothers, 1911, pp. 272–73.

across the Pacific consumed most of July as well. Not until the 25th of that month, fifty-five days after Dewey's naval victory, did Major General Wesley Merritt, the expedition commander, arrive at Cavite.

That Santiago surrendered July 16, Manila on August 12, the day after a protocol ending hostilities was signed in Washington, was rather an index of Spanish blunders than of American brilliance. Soldiers and sailors both fought in the tradition established by their forebears at Valley Forge and Lundy's Lane. But many of their hardships were needlessly imposed by the mistakes of their own country, as on those earlier fields.

The detailed records, so briefly sketched here, as well as the stories of the short campaigns in Cuba and Luzon should have registered a memorable lesson upon a nation which even then annually moved 142 billion ton-miles of freight, manufactured 10,000,000 tons of steel.[16] Yet the glaring disparity between our industrial and military technologies roused more interest in Europe than at home. Cynical diplomats shrugged off their amazement with the adage: "A guardian angel watches over the footsteps of drunkards and the United States of America."

It was left for the Army's commanding general to officially and quite inaccurately inscribe the epilogue, expressing his belief that "the experience will be valuable to the people and Government of the United States." He compounded the confusion on defense strategy when he added the hope that "the System of Coast Defenses . . . urged in my annual reports for 13 years . . . may be carried out without unnecessary delay."[17]

[16] *Historical Statistics of the U.S.*, Government Printing Office.

[17] Annual Report, General Miles, November 1898, p. 37.

As events of the twentieth century demonstrated, General Miles was wrong on both counts. By 1914, American steel production, now 23,000,000 tons annually, had been called upon to provide only 1300 guns, two-thirds of which were, by that date, obsolete.[18] It is an ironic footnote that during this decade, American military leaders, although aided by observation of the Russo-Japanese War, did not realize that fortified harbors were impotent unless guarded by mobile ground forces able to contest landing beaches on their flanks. Advances in transportation, afloat and ashore, although outstripping their utilization by the military—not only in the United States—made field armies, not fixed harbor emplacements, the real defenders of coast lines. Identical stagnation would also become apparent, in the pitiless glare of national emergency, in the techniques of organization, communications and the conversion of industry to support the military establishment.

World Power

With these military characteristics, the country entered the twentieth century. Our military struggled against public and congressional apathy to obtain men and funds for time-tested procedures and weapons. Innovation received slight attention from the military in an environment where the least items essential to survival must be wrung from an indifferent nation. Scientists and industry generally confined their efforts to peaceful endeavors, while such exceptions as the Wright Brothers and Hudson Maxim went to Europe for appreciative audiences.

[18] House Committee on Military Affairs, Hearings on Army Appropriations bill for 1916, p. 612.

The United States had suddenly emerged as a world power based upon its technology no less than its abundant resources. Our people and few among our leaders appreciated, if they were indeed aware of it, their nation's new position. On the surface, nothing seemed to have changed. The infusion of superior technology into the military establishment and even its import as a base for national policies were ignored for a complex variety of reasons.

CHAPTER II

EVE OF WAR

DURING THE RELATIVELY BRIEF SPAN FROM 1900–14, TECH-
nology advanced at an accelerating tempo, both at home and
in Europe. Undoubtedly the most far-reaching development
was man's long-sought achievement of powered flight, first
firmly established by Wilbur and Orville Wright at Kitty
Hawk in North Carolina in December 1903. Samuel P.
Langley's efforts on the Potomac River the same year had
resulted in failure.

Although the Navy's Board of Construction denied Langley financial assistance, contending that the airplane "per-
tains strictly to the land service and not to the Navy,"[1] and
the Wright Brothers were privately financed, the Army encouraged aviation progress by scheduling flight trials for aircraft. Machines which would fly one hour, attain a maximum
speed of 40 miles per hour and carry two men, would be
purchased.

Forty-one designers entered, but on the test day at Fort

[1] *Navy Wings*, U. S. Navy Dept., NAVPERS 10822-A, Government
Printing Office, 1955, p. 3.

Myer, Virginia, September 17, 1908, only the Wright machine performed, proving its capabilities before its propeller blade failed. The resulting crash injured Orville Wright, the pilot, and killed Lieutenant Thomas E. Selfridge who accompanied him. Despite the accident, this flight surpassed all European achievements until, in July 1909, Louis Bleriot flew across the English Channel from Calais to Dover, initiating a frenzied international competition for aviation patents and records.

Aviation's Fledgling Wings

By 1910 the Navy, reversing its original stand, sponsored a Curtiss plane and pilot in the first successful launching of an airplane from a ship, the cruiser *Birmingham*, fitted with an 83-foot wooden platform.

Early the next year, the same pilot, Eugene Ely, landed his airplane on a ship, employing hooks and lines tautened by sandbags on a 120-foot platform to suggest a prototype of the aircraft carrier. The British Navy commissioned the first real carrier, the *Hermes*, in 1913. The U. S. Navy had to wait until 1922 for the *Langley*.

Glenn Curtiss also built and flew the first practical seaplane in January 1911, profiting by the failures of Henri Fabre (France) with "water-based" aircraft. An improved version, fitted with a scow-shaped pontoon and three-wheel landing gear, the world's earliest amphibian, was selected by the Navy as its initial aircraft purchase. Only a year later, Curtiss again led the field with a "flying boat," its engine and cockpit fitted into the redesigned pontoon. Developed into the flying boat, *America*, which was test flown in June 1914,

41

this craft was promptly purchased by the British government.

All these "firsts" were not only victories of American technology in general but in particular of the initiative and small-scale financing of the military services. Unfortunately, neither the Taft administration nor Congress seriously concerned themselves with the growth of this lusty technological infant. The first naval aviator, Lieutenant T. G. Ellyson, was trained at "no expense to the government" by the Curtiss Company at San Diego, since the Navy received only $25,000 from Congress (and that not until 1911) to buy three airplanes. Appropriations the following year for Army aviation were $100,000, one-fifth of the Secretary of War's request submitted three years previously.

By 1913, only four short years after Bleriot's Channel exploit, Europe had in many respects so far surpassed U.S. civilian and military aviation technology that a few U.S. technical observers were sent abroad for training. The extent to which we had lost our initial lead in military aviation appears in simple statistics. At the outbreak of World War I, the French Army possessed 300 planes with the other warring nations close behind. Two and a half years later when we entered the war, the U. S. Army had only 55 planes, all obsolete or obsolescent types, and 35 trained pilots. Naval data showed 45 seaplanes, 6 "flying boats" and a roster of 38 pilots (Navy and Marines).

Military Achievements

The record suggests that at least during the infancy of aviation the U.S. military had done well with insignificant resources. In addition to the technical progress cited, Army officers had tested, in October 1911, a bombsight and bomb-dropping device, invented by Riley E. Scott. A handful of military pilots had experimented with firing rifles and Lewis machine guns from airplanes at ground targets and taken photographs with the first makeshift aerial camera. More remarkable was a successful demonstration of two-way, ground-air radio communication by Lieutenants Dargue and Mauborgne,[2] resulting from experiments in radio begun in 1907. Although the "Aviation Section of the Signal Corps" which consisted of 60 officers and 260 enlisted men was not legally established until July 1914, the Army's Signal Corps had devoted constant attention to flight technology.

Congress under the leadership of Chairman James Hay, of the House Committee on Military Affairs, though chary with financial support, promptly discussed the military future of aviation. A proposal to establish an Air Corps as an independent line component of the Army[3] was rejected. The testimony included the statement of a young aviator, Captain (later Brigadier General) William Mitchell, that the proposal would retard development of military flying.

As the years of peace vanished into an era of precarious neutrality, America impassively observed the accelerated rate of foreign technology in the air. Under the impetus of war, French, German, and British designers and engineers all utterly outclassed us in quality as well as quantity. Anthony Fokker's (German) single-seater fighter aircraft with fixed machine guns synchronized to fire through the propeller entered combat in the summer of 1915. Early the next year it

[2] T. H. Greer, *Military Affairs*, Vol. XX, No. 4, January 1957.
[3] Ibid.

43

was surpassed by the faster (110 mph) French Nieuport XXIII.

Britain produced the De Havilland series of fighters and the Handley Page bombers, although Italy, with the Caproni, led in the somewhat neglected bomber types. By 1917, no really "modern" aircraft existed in America. We lacked even farsighted scientists such as Britain's F. W. Lanchester[4] whose able professional writing stirred both public and officialdom into activity. There was no American equivalent of Britain's Royal Aircraft Factory at Farnsborough which had set the pace for British industry and, prior to 1914, had freely exchanged technical data with its commercial rivals.

Technology's Doldrums

In the many other expanding technologies of the early twentieth century, our military establishment appears to have had little influence and less leadership. The field of transportation found this country abreast of, or leading, European nations qualitatively, our railroad trackage jumped from 259,000 miles in 1900 to 387,000 in 1914,[5] with heavier, faster rolling stock and locomotives. Freight tonnage had risen to 740 million tons for an average haul of almost 400 miles. Passenger mileage had reached 35 billion. Yet so poorly was this advancing civilian technology adapted to military needs, that concentration of an extemporized division at San Antonio, Texas, in March 1911, required weeks.

Intended to bolster the Army's weak border patrols as the violence of Mexico's civil war increased, the force consisted

[4] F. W. Lanchester, *Aircraft in Warfare*, Constable Ltd., London, 1916.

[5] *Historical Statistics of the U.S.*, Government Printing Office.

of three brigades of Infantry, one of Field Artillery, and one of Cavalry. At that time the Army possessed no divisional organization, even on paper. Some 12,000 of the 19,000 authorized strength had arrived from a number of scattered posts after six weeks, the final shortage being due to lack of personnel not railroad facilities. A separate but simultaneous troop movement brought 36 companies of Coast Artillery to Galveston to form a Special Brigade which did attain its scheduled maximum of 4000 men.

The ineptness of this unplanned rail deployment contrasts sharply with an analogous test of American rail transport half a century earlier: the emergency dispatch of re-enforcements to General William S. Rosecrans in September 1863, after his defeat at Chickamauga. Less than twelve days sufficed for the flimsy Civil War railroads to transport General Joseph Hooker's 23,000 men from their Virginia camps to Tennessee, a distance of 1200 miles. That exploit saved Rosecrans' army and won the astonished envy of European military staffs.

For its mission as mobile reserve the Maneuver Division, as it was designated, relied upon horses, mules, and wagons although motor vehicle production on a significant scale began in this decade. An impractical curiosity in 1900, when only 8000 passenger cars were registered in the whole country, the automobile had by 1914 developed into an important means of transport with 1,700,000 cars and 100,000 trucks in operation. American models, passenger and commercial, were cheaper and more numerous than their European counterparts. Progenitors of our mass production lines (notably the Ford Model T) outsold the costly, largely hand-produced foreign output.

Yet the U.S. military establishment lagged behind industry in appreciating the impending impact of the internal combustion engine. In sharp contrast with its prompt interest in faster airplanes and long-standing attention to Cavalry remount breeding, the Army neglected motor vehicle development. As late as 1913 the Quartermaster Corps was still testing improved mule-drawn wagons. The annual International Speedway competitions at Indianapolis which opened in 1909 as the culmination of nationwide road and track competitions attracted no attention in War Department circles. Foreign armies, faced with scarcer, more expensive vehicles, conducted conservative experiments, while French and German officers participated in automobile racing with official approval and the British War Office began buying American-made Fords.

Steel and the Military

Relationships between the military and the steel industry, comprising some of the most important contacts between civilian and military technologies, were equally hit and miss. Though a modest factor in the industry's over-all tonnage, military interests varied from naval ship construction to Army Ordnance. The insignificant procurement of heavy guns for coast defenses has been noted. Artillery shells, cast from steel instead of iron after 1890, absorbed relatively few tons. Most of the military's purchases went into the steel consumed in naval building programs. In 1914 our fleet ranked third in the world, its eight battleships outnumbered by Britain's 34 and Germany's 21 capital ships. Nevertheless, in terms of national effort, steel's participation in U.S. defense was only marginal, since Britain and Germany together produced only two-thirds as much steel as the United States. Pointedly justified was Homer Lea's technological criticism in 1909: "Japan constructs a 20,000 ton battleship of the new type in two years. In the United States it requires over five years to build one of 16,000 tons."[6]

Nor were the military's customer relations with the steel industry all that could be desired. No small amount of Congressional opposition to naval expansion arose from disclosure that the newly formed Steel Trust charged the Navy half again as much for armor plate as for identical items delivered abroad. This behavior by an industry profiting from tariff protection and government contracts continued to rankle until Secretary of the Navy Josephus Daniels in the Wilson administration brought the trust to terms.

A smaller manifestation of government dissatisfaction with American steel manufacturers appears in the partially competitive operations of the Naval Gun Factory in Washington which carried on highly specialized steel work. In a closely related area, the Army was authorized in 1906 to manufacture powder at its Picatinny Arsenal, Dover, New Jersey, partly to insure uniform quality among different lots of explosive, but also to apply a brake on industry's prices. Two years later, Picatinny's output of 500 pounds per day represented six per cent of national production. For some years thereafter, Congressional appropriations for the Army specified a maximum price that might be paid per pound for powder, setting one of the earliest, though little noticed, precedents in price fixing.

Germany employed quite different methods in an early example of large-scale utilization of economic strength for mili-

[6] *Valor of Ignorance*, Homer Lea, Harper's 1909 (cf. Soviet/U. S. Construction time for long range bombers, half a century later).

tary purposes. The surge of German steel production to almost 11,000,000 tons annually, supported by governmental subsidies, doubled Britain's output by 1908. Expanded to an uneconomic degree for peacetime commerce, Germany's steel industry met wartime military requirements that would have been impossible save for the German Empire's calculated policy of overproduction.

The unfortunate experiences of the U.S. military in transportation and steel were repeated in the many other fields where civilian and military technologies might have cooperated to a much greater extent. Public indifference to War and Navy Departments requests for funds and facilities, reflected in Congressional frugality, marked the military as more sinned against than sinning. Harassed as it was in maintaining bare operating standards, the Army may be charged with some lack of vision. The Navy, with relatively larger budgets, managed to devote slightly greater attention to technological development.

There are solid grounds nevertheless for Dupree's[7] comment that the old scientific spirit of the early nineteenth century had almost disappeared from the armed services except for some enclaves of research like the Naval Observatory and the Army Medical Department. Gone, too, was the wilderness exploration that once had nurtured that spirit. Now, however, there were signs of a new awakening. The "first rustlings of weapons research in the services"[7] could be faintly heard. For example, Bradley A. Fiske, an 1874 Naval Academy graduate, repaid his leave of absence to study electrical engineering by filing some 60 patents prior to World War I. The Army Signal Corps, which had founded

[7] *Science in the Federal Government*, A. H. Dupree, Belknap Press of Harvard University Press, 1957, p. 302, 303.

a National Weather Service through the efforts of Colonel Albert J. Myer after the Civil War, showed the most energy and imagination in scientific matters, according to Dupree. That Corps' pioneering in aviation and radio are matters of record, supporting the Dodge Commission's earlier praise that the services of the Signal Corps had become of inestimable value.

In the realm of management, the Navy moved toward top-level co-ordination, wider in scope than traditional "command channels," by establishing the General Board (1900), with Admiral George Dewey as its first president. Directed to advise the Secretary of the Navy on war plans, fleet operations, ship construction, as urged by Admiral Mahan's disciples, the Board had to overcome opposition in Congress and from Bureau chiefs in the Navy. The Army sought the same goal via its General Staff, authorized by Congress in February 1903 after Secretary of War Elihu Root's three-year campaign overcame charges of militarism and the determined resistance of the Army's hitherto independent Bureau Chiefs. This act equipped the Army with a much more effective command structure than the Navy. The post of Chief of Naval Operations, roughly equivalent to the Army's Chief of Staff, was not created until 1915. Two more decades passed before the Navy's ranking officer was endowed with commensurate authority.

Genesis of Joint Planning

These new management agencies prepared the way for creating the Joint Army-Navy Board, first formal instrument of Army and Navy co-ordination on strategic problems. The

49

Board's eight members came equally from the General Staff and the Navy Board. After their early deliberations had brought about the fortification of Corregidor, begun in 1906, Army and Navy co-operation bogged down in a bitter argument concerning Philippine defense strategy.

Inability to decide between Manila and Subic Bay as the main U.S. base in the Philippines cost the Joint Board the confidence of President Theodore Roosevelt. His successor, William Howard Taft, practically ignored the still deadlocked Board which later incurred President Woodrow Wilson's displeasure in May 1913 by the alleged leakage (to the press) of Board findings on the indefensible state of our Pacific possessions. Thus, the potential value of sound managerial development was vitiated in political and personality clashes.

The military establishment met another reverse along similar lines when labor unions secured insertion of a provision in the Army Appropriations Act, Fiscal 1916, forbidding piecework under the economical Taylor System in certain arsenals. Frederick W. Taylor, a pioneer in scientific management practices, had been advising the Army on manufacturing processes so successfully that "various arsenals had effected considerable savings in the cost of production"[8] and justified a bonus to workers at the Watertown Arsenal.

One other Congressional enactment in the first years of the twentieth century, the Dick Bill[9] (January 1903), sharply portrays the extent of legislative neglect of military policy. The law repealed a 1792 statute and made the first Federal mention of the National Guard, the more important cate-

[8] Report of the Secretary of War, 1913, pp. 25–28.

[9] Introduced by Senator Charles Dick, Ohio.

gory among state troops known generally as militia. Although this force's organization and equipment was at last ordered to be the same as the Regular Army the new act added little to national defense. State governors could still refuse to call the Guard into service (as three did in the War of 1812) and the maximum term of service was restricted to only nine months. Elihu Root, seeking a stronger law, declared: "It is absurd that a nation which depends upon unprofessional citizen soldiery for its defense should run along 110 years under a militia law which never worked."[10] However, the Dick Bill may be regarded as forerunner of the Federalized National Guard (1916) and the latter's notable service to the nation.

Military Problems of Peace

Americans of the decade preceding World War I had few contacts with and less knowledge of their Army. If they thought of it at all they vaguely bracketed the Regular Army somewhere between loafers and martinets training for the remote contingency of war. Too many had seen the small detachments of Regulars who responded to state governors' appeals to "restore order" after natural disasters or more frequently in labor disturbances. Workers and their sympathizers not unnaturally castigated the Army for carrying out this unwelcome role. The normally fair-minded president of the American Federation of Labor, Samuel Gompers, speaking in Boston at the turn of the century had charged that "standing armies are always used to exercise tyranny over the people."

[10] *Elihu Root*, by Philip C. Jessup, Dodd Mead & Co., 1937.

When called to assist or temporarily replace civilian authorities at disaster scenes, e.g., the San Francisco earthquake, forest fires, Mississippi Valley floods, . . . far greater Army exertions attracted slight notice. So too, infrequent field maneuvers, with a few hundred Regulars joining more sizable National Guard contingents, drew public interest to about the extent accorded an itinerant circus.

Probably not one American in a thousand thought of the clannish, tiny Regular Army in connection with national security. The military problems of the United States seemed, to intelligent contemporary observers, no greater than maintaining a Navy capable of protecting our shores; an Army adequate to maintain order in the Philippines, garrison Panama, and provide a nucleus for mobilizing our traditional citizen-soldier forces.

The military profession was held in such low esteem that Congress found it necessary to affirm the rights of individuals in uniform. A 1911 act imposed a $500 fine upon proprietors of public places who denied soldiers the services normally rendered to any civilian. But Secretary Root was unable to block a law prohibiting beer at post canteens, which imposed the forerunner of prohibition bigotry upon the Army. Navy Secretary Daniels himself applied the same treatment to the Navy ten years later.

Yet the Army of reality bore little resemblance to popular beliefs. The Army actually had little time to train and its facilities and funds were utterly inadequate to train with. The foremost handicap to efficient training was, according to a 1910 survey, the Army's dispersal among 700 posts averaging less than 700 men each. Unaccountably, the isolated Fort D. A. Russell (later Fort Francis E. Warren for the Wyoming Senator and chairman of the Senate Military Affairs

Committee) near Cheyenne, Wyoming, housed the largest garrison of any.

The origin of many of these military posts lay in some forgotten campaign against hostile Indians. Few were abandoned although their tactical role had vanished and their distance from other posts and from suitable training areas was remote. William Howard Taft, War Secretary following Root, recommended the consolidation of scattered posts to facilitate maneuvers, economize on maintenance. Congress took no action, nor did Taft as President support his own Secretary of War, Jacob M. Dickinson, in a similar plea three years later. In the following year, the General Staff submitted a plan to combine Regulars and Guards into a three division field army. Not only were the funds necessary to test the plan in field maneuvers refused but President Taft so far reversed his former position as to publicly rebuke Secretary Dickinson and General Leonard Wood, Army Chief of Staff. Taft declared the United States defense system was entirely sufficient without alteration.

The Stimson Plan Encounters Politics

In the closing months of Taft's administration Henry L. Stimson, Dickinson's successor, submitted a four-point program to modernize the Army committed to his charge. Stimson sought to create a favorable climate of public opinion by a series of magazine articles prepared by officers and climaxed with his own views that the Army's deficiencies were caused by the lack of an intelligent military policy. His plan urged: (a) organized Infantry divisions and Cavalry brigades, (b) an active Reserve for the Regular Army, (c) a Reserve Officer program, and (d) trained citizen soldiers to reinforce the Regulars.

Neither Stimson's personal prestige nor the General Staff's painstaking preparation won noticeable support. The minority favoring a stronger posture of national defense had their hands full protecting the Navy's building program. In a short time the onset of the strenuous three-sided presidential campaign (Wilson-Roosevelt-Taft) wholly engrossed America. Stimson's efforts to make the U. S. Army somewhat more appropriate to the technologically advanced nation it sought to guard proved fruitless like those of all his predecessors since Elihu Root. Then, after a dozen lean years under Presidents at least reputedly friendly to the military establishment, the Army encountered the Wilson administration, which began with a policy that almost amounted to pacifism. The nearest the Democratic platform of 1912 approached a plank on military policy was a statement favoring retention of naval stations in the Philippines.

But the years before Wilson had not wholly bypassed the Army. Not only had Elihu Root accomplished the tremendous forward step of legalizing a General Staff, he had revitalized the Army school system with the newly authorized Army War College at the top of the pyramid. The Command and Staff College at Fort Leavenworth, Kansas, founded as a School of Application for Cavalry and Infantry by General Sherman (1881), was reopened in 1902. Among its graduates were to be listed most of the successful commanders of two World Wars. Supporting these higher level schools, the several arms and services of the Army established their own graduate institutions in futherance of Root's broad vision.

Root's Reforms Make Progress

A lesser man than Secretary Root, who had been chosen by Theodore Roosevelt for his task in 1899, could not have won Congressional approval of the General Staff system opposed then and since by many Americans as a symbol of abhorred militarism. Lord Haldane, Britain's great war minister called Root's five annual departmental reports "the very last word concerning the organization and place of an army in a democracy."[11]

Root saw the inefficiencies and mismanagement of the Spanish-American War in the light of a huge corporation without a general manager. There was, for example, no one charged with ascertaining whether the artillery found Ordnance furnished matériel satisfactory; no one to see that facilities existed at Tampa to handle the trainloads of men and supplies dispatched to that port.

Urging a General Staff to provide management and planning functions in conformance with his corporation model, Root simultaneously sought to guard against two potential evils of that system. Any tendency to overload the Staff with administrative details was to be avoided. At the other extreme, a Staff hierarchy, ignorant of or insensible to the needs of the troops, was prevented. General Staff assignments were filled without exception by selected line officers, each of whom must return to service with troops after a four-year Staff detail. This last provision ensured a sharp distinction between a democratic nation's agency for military manage-

11 *Elihu Root* by Philip C. Jessup, Dodd Mead & Co., 1937, Vol. I, p. 227.

ment and the German Imperial General Staff of permanent careerists. To this day much antagonism to the General Staff system is based upon ignorance of this distinction.

One year after the General Staff began its duties in 1903, the War Department held the first joint field maneuvers for Regulars and Guardsmen. Nearly 10,000 of the former and over 30,000 state troops took part at three locations, in California, Washington, and Virginia. Although Congress withheld maneuver funds in 1905 a $700,000 allocation the next year financed seven camps of instruction. The 20,000 Regulars who participated comprised almost every available soldier in the busy year of 1906 when the bulk of General Frederick Funston's West Coast command had their work cut out for them for three months in San Francisco assisting after the earthquake and fire. Army supplied "rations" and tents fed and housed thousands while order was restored by soldier patrols.

Meanwhile an insurrection in Cuba brought an appeal for U.S. assistance from the president of that new republic. A well-equipped expedition of over 5000 Regulars embarked at once from Gulf ports. The prompt arrival of this strong force ended the fighting although the so-called Cuban Pacification "Campaign" lasted for two years as a police measure.

The report of the Secretary of War credits the General Staff with marked improvement over conditions in 1898. One thing however was beyond the capability of the staff: there had been insufficient ships flying the American flag to transport the troops to Cuba. Fortunately foreign vessels had been available for prompt charter.

Big Navy, Small Support

If the nation noticed the embarrassment of being compelled to rely upon hired transports to move even a small expeditionary force no remedial action was taken. Nor did the embarrassment remotely approach that suffered by the Navy a year later. President Roosevelt dispatched the sixteen battle ships of the U. S. Fleet on a world cruise (Dec. 1907–Feb. 1909), to serve notice that the U.S. would tolerate no breach of the peace.

Actually, to naval experts the "Great White Fleet" on its voyage of circumnavigation presented a "melancholy and foreboding spectacle; sixteen American warships in convoy with 28 chartered vessels flying a foreign flag without which they could not have steamed beyond the sphere of their Atlantic bases."[12] The "big Navy" men, headed by the retiring President, ignored the absurdity of a "single shot" battle line devoid of supporting ships, but at least the admirals gained experience in Long-range logistics. (Despite these unheeded embarrassments it was not until the Hepburn Board in 1939 termed the U. S. Navy incapable, for lack of bases and sea-train, of fighting more than one engagement at sea that Congress created the office of Undersecretary of the Navy to put naval logistics in combat readiness.)

While the Fleet voyaged, a revolution in sea power occurred with the commissioning of Britain's *Dreadnought*, the first all-big-gun, fast battleship. By the time the Fleet returned to Hampton Roads and "Teddy's" enthusiastic welcome, every ship in its battle line was obsolete. England had

[12] Op. Cit., Homer Lea.

57

the "Orion" class superdreadnoughts, carrying larger than 12-inch guns, under construction.

In this country the Navy Department sought vainly to impress Congress with the significance of these momentous technological advances. A frenzied naval armament race had begun in Europe. Britain's pre-dreadnought warships were now as useless as those of all other nations. Germany, seizing the chance to overtake her rival, drew upon her accumulated stocks of steel for naval construction.

The prospect had been faced with foreboding but determination by the British Admiralty which wrought the revolution. Practically all existing naval drydocks were useless, yards had to be rebuilt. In Germany the Kiel Canal, a wholly military project to unite the Baltic and North Seas fleets, had to be enlarged to pass such ships. The Panama Canal, then under construction, was not to face the same problem until the day of the supercarriers.

For this country the timing proved especially unfortunate. During his seven years as President, Theodore Roosevelt had fought hard to build a powerful Navy. Now, under President Taft, the job must be redone, more expensively, against stronger opposition. Senator Eugene Hale of Maine, Chairman of the Naval Affairs Committee, withdrew his support and voiced strange sentiments for a statesman in his position: "Every immense appropriation for a war establishment increases the chances for war."[13] The National Association of Manufacturers denounced naval armament, declaring that commerce was a better guarantor of peace. Nevertheless two ships of the *Delaware* class, roughly equaling Britain's dreadnoughts, received approval as this country's initial venture into modern battleships. By the time World War I broke out we had eight, England four times as many.

[13] Congressional Record, 61st Congress, 2nd Session, 6595.

Nothing like the intensity of the debate over naval building programs touched the Army. A Board studying coast defenses in 1905–06 with War Secretary William H. Taft as chairman, took pains to differentiate between a true coastal defense system and mere harbor protection. Costs to complete a modern program for the latter, including the terminals of the Panama Canal, were set at $50,000,000. Only a strong mobile Army could insure coast defense. No one argued with the Board's findings or took the slightest action to implement them, other than a $3,000,000 allotment for fortifications in Panama.

During these years, strictly within its own house, the Army developed the Springfield rifle, the best weapon in its class for a generation but failed to equal the French field artillery and could not agree on a standard machine gun. A Board at Rock Island Arsenal, expected to devise new infantry equipment, only came up with a new infantry pack. Yet despite this spotty technological performance the engineering problems of constructing the Panama Canal were entrusted to Colonel George W. Goethals and a handful of Army Engineers when President Roosevelt came to the conclusion that no civilian agency could handle it.

The Wilson Paradox

This ambiguous attitude of reliance upon the military coincident with general indifference to their requirements became more pronounced under Wilson's administration. The new President's policy paradoxically did not preclude expanded employment of the nation's armed forces although it emphatically opposed strengthening them for the tasks imposed.

During the tension with Japan, caused by California's alien land bill, the Joint Army-Navy Board reported the defenseless state of American possessions in the Pacific and incurred President Wilson's wrath as has been noted in Chapter 1. Its recommendations were ignored.

The two thousand Marines sent to suppress a revolt in Nicaragua in 1912 during the Taft administration were retained there under a treaty negotiated by William Jennings Bryan, Wilson's pacifist Secretary of State. Marines and sailors sufficed to occupy Haiti and Santo Domingo but the drawn-out involvement of the Army in Mexico was on the scale of a major effort.

The Mexican "campaign" entered its first phase April 22, 1914, when Rear Admiral Frank F. Fletcher's Atlantic Fleet, upon Presidential Order, captured Vera Cruz in a pitched battle to prevent delivery of German munitions to dictator Victoriano Huerta's forces. The action was taken in advance of Congressional approval to use the military, although the President's request had been sent to Congress. Incidently the battle marked the initial appearance of U.S. aircraft in combat when a navy hydroplane reconnoitered under fire for the landing force. This plane and two others, the Fleet's entire complement of aircraft, were deadlined by mechanical troubles within the week.

Army reinforcements, ordered the day after Vera Cruz fell, managed to embark a force of some 3000 infantry from Galveston in twenty-four hours, utilizing four Army transports forehandedly dispatched by the General Staff to that port. A battalion of artillery followed two days later. This superficially creditable record was marred by the fact that the available ships could not load much of the Army's mules and wagons. The expedition was consequently incapable of movement beyond the immediate neighborhood of Vera Cruz, where it stayed until recalled in November.

Nor was our relatively far more powerful Navy maintained ready for hostilities. During the Fleet's protracted stay in Mexican waters lack of **an** oceangoing supply train precluded target practice. The crews of the two newest battleships the *Texas* and the *New York* had never fired a gun.[14]

However, while the bulk of America's ready military forces were concerned with a petty undeclared war against a dictator in Mexico, revolts against Latin American despots (Nicaragua and Santo Domingo) and internal labor troubles, titanic military operations began in Europe.

Neutrality's Effect Upon Technology

The outbreak of war in Europe brought obvious threats to America's economic stability. Frantic sales of European securities closed the New York Stock Exchange on July 31, 1914. To prevent strangulation of American foreign trade, President Wilson hastened to Congress for authority to create a government-owned merchant marine.

Succeeding events quickly dispelled the threats. Prompt Treasury fiscal action supported by prominent banks averted a financial panic. The anticipated chaos in the sea lanes failed to materialize. (Congress restricted its action to relaxing ship registry laws and rejecting a Senate proposal to use naval vessels as cargo carriers.) Before long a rising tide of foreign purchases erased all danger of a business depression.

Threats to our national security remained obscure, how-

14 General Board to Secretary of the Navy, Sept. 9, 1914.

ever, subject to increasingly bitter debate for nearly three years of neutrality. The only early impact upon the military establishment was the dispatch of a few Army and Navy officers to Europe to assist stranded American tourists.

A flurry of concern over the inadequate state of national defense, lead by Theodore Roosevelt, roused bitter antagonism among progressives, labor and peace groups. Representative Augustus P. Gardner of Massachusetts failed in an attempt to force a Congressional investigation of Army and Navy readiness. Secretary Daniels ignored the advice of his General Board and declared the Navy in "fine shape." President Wilson scoffed at "nervous and excited people" in his December message to Congress and a month later, without opposition from Congressional leaders, ordered the military budgets cut as an answer to what he termed "a lobby stirring artificial alarm."[15]

In the spring of 1915, events added impetus to the preparedness movement, still a pronounced minority. British blockade practices had already ignored the United States' traditional demand for freedom of the seas, but Germany's submarine warfare killed Americans, first one man (Leon C. Thrasher) when the British steamer *Falaba* was sunk; then 128 U.S. citizens and 1100 other passengers died on the *Lusitania*.

Books and magazines, even motion pictures,[16] began to fictionalize the invasion of America by helmeted, goosestepping armies that swept aside the ill-equipped defenders, undermining Secretary of State Bryan's boast that, in an emergency, "a million men would spring to arms overnight."

[15] Arthur S. Link, *Woodrow Wilson and the Progressive Era*, Harper & Brothers, 1954, p. 177.

[16] *The Battle Cry of Peace* and *The Fall of a Nation* drew large cinema audiences. Hudson Maxim's book *Defenseless America* lead the literary field.

Despite the hue and cry, however, the majority of Americans backed the antimilitarism policies of Congress set by House Majority Leader Claude Kitchin of North Carolina. Bryan resigned rather than take a firm stand against Germany. Representative Gardner's bill to raise a $3,000,000 appropriation for artillery ammunition to $35,000,000 was overwhelmingly rejected although only 5800 rounds,[17] half a day's expenditure in the Marne Battle, existed in the United States. About this time President Wilson evinced his anger toward the Army War College, then serving as a war plans division of the General Staff, for "preparing war plans against nations with which the U.S. is at peace."[18]

The military unpreparedness of the United States while Europe was in the grip of war has been repeatedly cited as preposterous disregard for our national safety. Statistics seem to justify the harshest criticism. By way of example, less than 40,000 troops, roughly twice the size of New York City's police force, comprised the mobile army in the United States after deducting overseas garrisons and coast artillery units. Even this small force was deficient in machine guns and artillery. The forts defending the Panama Canal had ammunition for only two hours' firing at battle expenditure rates. Although Germany commercially produced nitrate for explosives from nitrogen in the atmosphere, no such plant existed in America. We depended almost entirely upon imports from Chile.

Yet this situation was consistent with the American tradition of never recognizing a military emergency until one hit us. Despite the prevalence of preparedness propaganda por-

[17] About one-tenth the number fired, in the fall of 1958, by Chinese Communist batteries at the island of Quemoy.

[18] *Woodrow Wilson and the Progressive Era*, Arthur S. Link, Harper & Brothers, 1954, p. 168.

traying the conquest of this country by an invading army, the continental U.S.A. was in no more danger from German armies, or fleets, than it had been eight years earlier when Homer Lea's *Valor of Ignorance* detailed the "impending invasion by Japan."

Justified Civilian Incredulity

On that score, civilian incredulity proved sounder than the military's alarm. The impact of technological progress upon armies' and navies' combat capabilities did indeed render our small defense establishment impotent before those theoretical opponents. Yet the logistic technologies of warfare had not advanced anywhere near a point where either Japan or Germany (or indeed the two combined) could have mounted, much less supported, an invasion force strong enough to conquer so vast—and distant—a nation as the U.S.

Had the British Fleet suddenly vanished from the seas, the French and Russian armies ignominiously surrendered, Germany in 1914–16 might have seized large areas of our Atlantic Coast, as English armies did one hundred years before. Any serious belief that Germany could have maintained such forces, marched them to the Mississippi and the Great Lakes, vanishes upon examining the record of contemporary history. The German Empire managed to penetrate only 300 miles into dying Russia by January 1917, after two and a half years of war.

The American people might have surrendered rather than make the tremendous effort required to eject the invader—but our history marks that eventuality as remote. In over-all technology, Germany (or Japan) was no match for the U.S. in the twentieth century's second decade although each had directed greater shares of their technology into military channels. Had the Kaiser's forces been handicapped by a 3000-mile line of communications while we fought on our hearthstones, the impetus of greater urgency felt by every citizen would have permitted American counterthrusts, despite American confusion and territory lost, long before this imaginary invasion threatened our vitals.

Men like "Teddy" Roosevelt and Henry L. Stimson realized, however, that the forces edging the U.S. into World War I were strategic in nature. Their motivation was a far-sighted recognition that our long-range security depended upon preventing the domination of Europe by a military empire hostile to this country. Thus began a strategic policy debate which has repeatedly, in fact almost continuously, confused our military policy ever since. Preparedness proponents in 1915–16 resorted to fear psychology rather than confront the nation with the more complex, real problem. Whether their failure to take the public into their confidence strengthened or weakened their program and whether the strategic issue could have been popularly understood would be a case study in democracy under stress. A useful corollary might analyze the influence of "scare propaganda" in producing the isolationist surge two decades later.

Industry Discovers War Profits

While military decisions hung fire, U.S. industry was acquiring, in 1915–16, some incidental readiness for war through the medium of Allied purchases. No government agency, civilian or military, made the slightest attempt to co-ordinate this war production. American businessmen, notably Charles M. Schwab of Bethlehem Steel and J. P. Morgan, naturally sought profits. The House of Morgan opened negotiations for a $100,000,000 loan to France in August 1914 though State Department objections delayed transactions more than a year. Eventually, the Morgan firm floated 80 per cent of the two and one half billion dollars of Allied loans, or "credits" as they were termed, advanced by private investors in this country during 1915–16.

Details of Mr. Schwab's activities remain obscure to this day. Hastening to England in October 1914 he consulted Lord Kitchener, Britain's War Minister. Thereafter Bethlehem Steel converted its production largely to munitions though data on the items produced is vague. British authorities later praised Schwab for building ten submarines in five months, compared to a normal 14 month construction period. These warships, of the advanced "H" class, were apparently assembled in Canada from Bethlehem's fabricated materials, and in the spring of 1915 became the first undersea craft in history to cross the Atlantic under their own power en route to join Britain's Dardanelles expedition. The entire matter was handled with such secrecy that not until November did the German ambassador in Washington protest an alleged breach of neutrality.

American industry was more competitive than its bankers. The 1914 depression disappeared in an avalanche of Anglo-French orders, chiefly for metal products, chemicals, and explosives, that exceeded two billions of dollars by March 1917. Barely $10 millions were spent in the decrepit American aviation industry. A diversified trade with the Netherlands and Scandinavia spiraled to a 300 per cent increase, amounting to $200 millions in the first six months of 1915. By midsummer the tightening British blockade system rapidly strangled these latter exports but the protests of aggrieved shippers went unheard amidst the din of mounting purchases by England and France.

This wholly unplanned, indirect contribution to our defense potential was characteristic. Congress evidenced foresight in scientific matters by the creation in 1915 of the National Advisory Council on Aeronautics, recognizing the necessity of government leadership in developing this new frontier of science. Its twelve members included two Army and two Navy representatives. Yet a few weeks earlier the same Congress soundly defeated Representative Gardner's amendment to the Army Appropriation Bill, which asked for a modest $1,300,000 increase for military aircraft.

In July 1915, the Navy Department revived, after a fifty-year lapse, a Naval Consulting Board emulating Secretary Gideon Welles' Civil War precedent. This pioneering effort toward modern research and development concepts proposed expert evaluation of ideas received from inventors, civilian and military.[19] Acting without Congressional authority or funds, Secretary Daniels appointed Thomas A. Edison as Board Chairman. His request for $8,000,000 for a naval laboratory under military command to employ "civilian experimenters operating in secrecy" was cut to one million. Although the outbreak of war canceled the project, today's Naval Research Laboratory, established in 1923, may be regarded as the logical outgrowth of the attempt.

[19] The Board's war record shows some 100,000 suggestions received, about 100 deemed worthy of detailed examination and one put into production. This low payoff from random enthusiasm serves as a milestone on the slowly learned lesson; military research requires teamwork, combining experience in operational as well as scientific skills.

War's Lessons Go Unheeded

Outside of these valuable beginnings, military problems were ignored by the various scientific bureaus of the government whose potential, like that of university and industrial laboratories remained untapped. Even the military itself may seem to have slighted some of its few professional opportunities. Events of the Russo-Japanese War had been observed at firsthand by officers soon to become prominent, notably: John J. Pershing; Peyton C. March, wartime Chief of Staff; Joseph E. Kuhn, later president of the War College; Enoch H. Crowder, future administrator of the draft law; John F. Morrison, major general in War Department plans by 1917. Hard facts, not theories, emerged from the barbed wire and trench lines in depth at Port Arthur; the Japanese use of the Hotchkiss machine gun; both armies' dependence upon heavy artillery. All these forecast the setting for greater battles in Europe. Especially noteworthy for ocean-ringed America were Japan's landing operations and oversea supply lines. At sea, the effectiveness of mines, the value of battleship speed replacing Nelson's famed "weather gauge" were equally prophetic. Looking still farther ahead one might have been impressed by Nipponese tactics of crippling the enemy fleet first and declaring war afterward. However, the officers who watched these operations did not reach positions of authority prior to World War I. During the years of wavering neutrality they were engrossed in assigned tasks. Long-range planning, much less an opportuntity to put plans into practice, has never been a strong element of our military policy.

For that matter, Europe's far more powerful military establishments fell short of excellence in professional vision. None of the warring nations had foreseen the extensive munitions industry required to produce the huge quantities of ammunition. Their armies began the war with few more machine guns per regiment than the four allotted to U.S. units. The stress of war did not eliminate foolish rejection of decisive new weapons. The story of Winston Churchill as Britain's First Sea Lord rescuing the land service's "tank" from oblivion is well known. Relatively simple technical problems of mating farm machinery's endless track propulsion to the armored car proved far easier than convincing generals of the scheme's tactical utility. In Germany, the chemist Franz Huber vehemently opposed by Army generals on tactical, *not* moral grounds, won permission to achieve only a local victory. His brain child, the April 1915 gas attack at Ypres, might have been a decisive breakthrough. Nor were navies more prescient. Neither Britain nor Germany foresaw the real potential of submarine warfare, either offensively or defensively.

Such examples could be cited endlessly without altering their theme. Nations, not merely soldiers, have been guilty of preparing for the next war in the image of the last. But a return to the political scene in America during the summer of 1915 seems more rewarding.

Wilson Endorses "Preparedness"

President Wilson's determination to send a "strong" note of protest over the sinking of the *Lusitania* caused Bryan to resign from the Cabinet. The administration's veiled threat to sever diplomatic relations unless Germany modified her submarine operations intensified the divided state of opinion in America. Wilson quietly asked the War and Navy Secretaries for plans to strengthen national defense, a surprising reversal of his previous stand and the first open expression of concern by a U. S. President, in time of peace, over the weakness of our military establishment.[20]

After several months of evasive diplomatic maneuverings, the German government promised, in August, to refrain from attacks on passenger ships. International tension relaxed but dissension at home reached a new pitch with the clarification of the President's conversion to preparedness. In a New York speech on November 4, 1915, Wilson accorded full support to the Navy's General Board plan to equal Britain's sea power in ten years, building $500 million worth of warships in the first five. Army General Staff requests, reduced by Secretary of War Lindley M. Garrison to what he believed obtainable, emerged as the "Continental Army" plan; a 40 per cent increase in the Regular Army to 142,000 men, establishing a 400,000 man reserve in three years, and abolishing the National Guard.

Preparedness advocates applauded while outraged foes of "militarism," a basic tenet of the Progressive movement that had elected Wilson, roared their disapproval. So formidable did Congressional opposition loom that the President undertook a tour of the Middle West where he defended preparedness as a nonpartisan national necessity. Results showed that the majority of workers and farmers remained unconvinced. By February Wilson's resolve weakened. He acquiesced in House Leader Kitchin's condemnation of the Army

[20] Theodore Roosevelt continuously hounded Congress for an "adequate," i.e., much bigger, Navy but never sought Army expansion.

Plan as a "symbol of uncontrolled militarism."[21] Garrison resigned, charging "little knowledge and very little intense interest in any of the members of the House concerning military affairs,"[22] a charge the President bluntly denied.

Opponents of the Navy program contented themselves with delaying tactics. Die-hard pacificists concentrated on the greater evil, Army expansion, aided until Garrison's defeat, by a strange ally, the powerful National Guard lobby.

Mexican Tryout

While the Capitol argued, events plunged the Army into active service on the Mexican border. In desperation over Washington's recognition of the Carranza regime, Pancho Villa's followers murdered foreigners in Chihuahua, including a score of U.S. citizens. When this desperate act failed to provoke American intervention, Villa raided into New Mexico. On March 9, 1916, the town of Columbus was burned and 19 citizens murdered.

President Wilson authorized an early version of "hot pursuit" and six days later Brigadier General Pershing led a column into Mexico to capture the raiders. By early April his force, now 7000 strong, had penetrated 200 miles of desolate country, watched suspiciously by four times his numbers of Carranzista troops. Although dispersed, Villa's band had evaded capture and Pershing's situation was precarious. Reports to the newly appointed War Secretary Newton D. Baker estimated Army strength insufficient to guarantee

[21] *Woodrow Wilson and the Progressive Era*, Arthur S. Link, p. 184.

[22] *Eight Years of Wilson's Cabinet*, David F. Horestone, Vol. I, 168.

Pershing's supply line or hold the border itself against an attack in force.

Within forty-eight hours after Pershing marched into Mexico, Congress authorized a Regular Army of 128,000, only 14,000 short of Garrison's rejected recommendation. So urgent was the need for men, the War Department had recruiting stations open before the bill was signed but failed to convince the administration that twice the authorized number of troops would scarcely ensure pacification of the Mexican guerrillas.

Abhorring war, Wilson's modest goal of a peaceful border needed Mexican co-operation. Instead it encountered Carranza's demand that U.S. forces withdraw immediately. Fortunately only one armed clash occurred during April. Forty Mexican soldiers and two of Pershing's men died near Parral but diplomatic negotiations conducted by Major General Hugh L. Scott and Mexican General Alvarado Obregón reached agreement on gradual withdrawal, an agreement accepted by Wilson but rejected by Carranza.

At this juncture Villa daringly attacked Glenn Springs, Texas, killing three soldiers and a civilian. Wilson ordered another pursuit column and Carranza threatened war at the end of May. The Mexican ultimatum touched off a General Staff directive to plan an invasion of Mexico along the rail lines and on June 18 the President invoked the brand new authority of the National Defense Act to call out the National Guard of all the states. Additional warships were sent to Mexican waters.

While the Guard mobilized, two troops of cavalry were defeated by a large Carranzista force at Carrizal. Captain Charles T. Boyd, Cavalry commander, and eleven men were killed, twenty-three were captured. The Mexican general and twenty-nine of his soldiers died in the battle. As

Wilson prepared a war message to Congress only news that Boyd had been the aggressor prevented war. Captain Lewis S. Morey, Boyd's second in command at Carrizal, reported his chief's order to attack in the expectation the Mexicans would run.

Actually less warlike than his words, Carranza promptly released the captured Americans. A Joint High Commission reaccomplished with diplomatic furbishes almost the identical truce agreement reached earlier by the military conferees. By the time Mexico again threatened to abrogate the truce, January 1917, the border was quiet. U.S. relations with Germany were rapidly deteriorating. Washington gave in at last and Pershing's columns started north before the month was out.

During the long months of the Mexican expedition Congress had finally enacted the first National Defense Act, prodded by happenings far from the Capitol. The Army was increased, in three annual increments, to 200,000, the National Guard to twice that figure in recognition of the embarrassment of being unable to protect our border from Mexican threats. A naval engagement in the North Sea influenced Navy appropriations still more drastically.

Jutland Alters Senate Votes

News of Jutland, the first sea battle of modern times between major fleets, reached Washington while the Senate debated. Realization that a German victory could have meant Allied defeat in the Great War[23] impressed the legislators with the risk of continuing to rely upon British sea

---

[23] Admiral Jellicoe's caution at Jutland was brusquely defended on the irrefutable grounds that he was "the only man who could have lost the War in one afternoon."

73

power for our defense. Naval technology was also strongly affected by the news which discredited the fast, lightly armored battle cruiser as a capital ship. Quickly the Senate approved the Navy Department building program but ordered it completed in three years, not five. With White House support the Senate version became law. Perhaps the act's most important provision recognized that modern war demanded "industrial mobilization" and empowered the President to seize private industry which failed to comply with orders for war materials.

In another concession to preparedness long advocated by the War Department, Congress created a Council of National Defense. Under the chairmanship of the Secretary of War, five other Cabinet members (Navy, Interior, Commerce, Agriculture, and Labor) comprised the Council. Provision was also made for a Civilian Advisory Commission of business and labor leaders to assist and advise. Baltimore and Ohio Railroad president Daniel Willard headed the Commission which included Samuel Gompers and Bernard Baruch, all pioneers of the famed "dollar-a-year" men who gave their services to the government in the war years. In this same spirit a group of civilian scientists instigated the formation of the National Research Council. Initially devoid of government support, the Council formed nation-wide committees of prominent scientists, financed by the Carnegie and Rockefeller Foundations, to represent the various branches of science. Little could be accomplished without official recognition and, as will be seen in Chapter III, the government had yet to formulate its ideas regarding the role of scientists in war.

But neither laws nor appropriations wrought swift improvement in our military establishment. The Navy was still to be built, the Army must be recruited and equipped. Nor did Congressional action imply a fundamental change in public opinion, slower to appreciate the situation. National elections returned Wilson to the presidency on the slogan "He kept us out of war." The keynote address of Martin H. Glynn, ex-governor of New York, at the Democratic National Convention in St. Louis drew little applause for praising Wilson's preparedness measures, but stumbled into an ovation by lauding "notewriting without recourse to war." Historian Arthur S. Link records that "it was as if the delegates discovered that pacifism, jeered at and derided, was the cornerstone of American foreign policy . . . a passion for peace deafened them to any other appeals."

In such an atmosphere the nation drifted, uncertain even as to its potential foe. As late as November 1916, Colonel Edward M. House warned the President that France and Britain, angered by our "peace without victory" suggestions, might declare war on the U.S. Wilson "doubted this but thought if they did they could do this country no serious hurt."[24] There was still no more real appreciation of the possibility that "American boys might be sent to fight in foreign wars" than was evident twenty-five years later.

The American public's idea of war remained fixed upon the possibility of a foreign assault upon our shores, remote, as it rightly seemed. Even resumption of Germany's unrestricted submarine warfare early in February 1917 brought only a break in diplomatic relations. Army leaders who suggested rapid preparation for war were abruptly told to mind their own business. The administration forbade the War Department to work on a conscription bill, and refused to employ the Navy on convoy duty to protect U.S. shipping in

[24] *Woodrow Wilson and the Progressive Era*, Arthur S. Link, p. 255.

the war zone. Congress passed the Army Appropriations Bill the same month without increase above its originally programed $250,000,000. Former Secretary of State William Jennings Bryan appealed to the people to pressure Congress to "keep the peace." Telegrams poured in from all sections of the land.

The disclosure of German intrigues in Mexico—the "Zimmerman notes" offering U.S. territory in return for Mexican attack on the United States—convinced the President that war was inevitable. When these were given to the press on March 1, after a Senate filibuster had blocked White House requests for authority to arm merchant shipping, editorial comment generally endorsed warlike preparations. Nevertheless, Congress adjourned on schedule suggesting as Wilson wrote his confidant, Colonel House: "The people do not wish to go to war, no matter how many Americans are lost at sea."

War Again

During March, U.S. ships were sunk without warning, first the *Algonquin*, by U-boat gunfire after the crew had escaped, then three more, the *Vigilancia*, *Illinois*, and *City of Memphis* all with loss of American lives. At this point the President acted. He called the National Guard back into Federal service; reconvened Congress and, on April 2, delivered his war message. Reversing the situation of 1898, the administration had, however reluctantly, committed the people, but in other respects, nothing had changed. Technological progress during thirty-two months of neutrality had left the United States still farther behind Europe in both military and industrial aspects of national defense. Exceptional achievements like Bethlehem Steel's submarine construction for Britain showed that latent capabilities existed. Programs such as the National Defense Act and the last-minute efforts of the Civilian Advisory Commission evidenced a belated awakening among America's leaders. Thus the world's foremost industrial nation, prepared, almost wholly on paper, stood on the brink of the greatest war in history, one that had already raged for nearly three years.

CHAPTER III

WAR'S LESSONS AT HOME AND ABROAD

AFTER THREE YEARS OF IMPASSIONED NEUTRALITY, THE United States became a belligerent in World War I one month and two days after Woodrow Wilson's second inauguration. Unlike all other major participants in that conflict, this country did not precede its declaration by mobilizing its military establishment on a war footing. In reality little or no force existed to be mobilized.

Although the original National Defense Act of 1916 had legalized a respectable Army and an "invincible" Navy, its provisions were scheduled to take effect so gradually that, by the spring of 1917, no appreciable increase in military strength had accrued. For example, Army enlistments, averaging 3000 per month, barely exceeded normal attrition. The nerve center of the War Department, the General Staff, was restricted by law to forty-four officers, of whom nineteen were on duty in Washington. This compared with 232 officers of similar function in Britain and the more than 600 each in Germany and France during the summer of 1914. By November 1918 our expanded "nerve center" contained 1000 officers, law or no law, but the number with prior General Staff experience had dropped to four.

Two fortuitous assets should, however, be taken into count. Nearly 75,000 National Guardsmen and half that number of Regulars, all the mobile army inside the continental U.S., had recently completed months of small unit training on the Mexican border. In addition, foreign orders to the tune of $3,000,000,000[1] had given birth to a heterogeneous munitions industry in this country. Conceived in haste and expediency, out of Allied need and American profit motives, that industry was an important adjunct to the Allies' war production. It was not intended to be, nor could it quickly become, in itself, the chief support of a balanced U.S. military establishment.

America Discovers Industrial Lead Time

Our traditional, though never justified, optimism regarding the combat prowess of hastily trained citizen-soldiers extended, in World War I, to belief in sheer miracles of technology and manufacture. This brash confidence was not restricted to those major fields of industry in which America already led the world. It was equally manifest in new developments, relatively unknown to U.S. industry. Perhaps the outstanding example may be found in aviation. Prior to April 1917, neither American industry nor military agencies had designed a single aircraft modern by World War I accelerated standards. Neither had we developed a powerful aircraft engine. Yet under pressures from our French Allies

[1] *A Diplomatic History of the American People*, T. A. Bailey, Crofts & Company, 1942.

and disregarding General Staff advice for a more balanced force the government promptly inaugurated a 25,000 plane program.[2]

Contentious studies of America's nineteen months' belligerency are so numerous that a mere bibliographical listing constitutes extensive research. For our purposes, the record is relatively simple and crystal clear. Immense production programs failed in only one critical detail, timing. Despite expenditure of a billion dollars to manufacture artillery pieces and ammunition, nearly every major item of modern munitions—and innumerable minor ones—failed to reach our forces in the theater of operations until after the Armistice. Some never became available even for training in this country. For example, of the 23,000 tanks on order, 26 had been completed by November 1918. To round out the cycle of waste, nearly all the rest were canceled.

Similarly, the two billion dollars poured into plane construction provided less than 700 aircraft, chiefly observation types plus a few copies of the British De Havilland 4 bomber and about one hundred H-16 flying boats from the Navy's aircraft factory in Philadelphia. No U.S.-built fighter aircraft reached the combat zone in France before hostilities ceased. U.S. aviators flew in Allied planes.

Right up to the Armistice, the majority of our troops reached Europe in British transports. U.S. armies went into battle with British or French artillery pieces; fired French manufactured artillery ammunition; manned French tanks. At the close of hostilities, 20,000,000 rounds of artillery ammunition had been manufactured in the U.S., twice the amount received from Allied sources. Three quarters of the

[2] *Wings of the Dawn*, E. E. Wilson, Connecticut Printer, Hartford, 1955, p. 71.

total came out of our factories after June 1918.[3] As an index to expenditure our Argonne offensive consumed over 4,000,000 rounds.

The Navy was equipped—and predominantly supplied—from sources within our nation although our warships in European waters were provisioned by Allied bases. The outstanding exception to the long list of U.S. mass production that came too late was shipping to defeat the U-boat menace. Our great ship-building surge had concentrated upon slow freighters and cargo tonnage, perhaps the war's most critical item, as events proved, came off the ways in unprecedented quantity beginning early in 1918.

Paradoxically, it was U.S. manpower, not matériel, that turned the tide of war against the Central Powers. This manpower was hastily, often inadequately, trained, but, strange as the phrase may sound more than forty years later, it was manpower imbued with a crusading zeal to fight. That was one of our two greatest contributions to the Allied cause. The second largely accounted for the first—clearly announced war aims that stirred the hearts, and minds, of men; aims "commensurate with the scale of suffering."[4]

Woodrow Wilson elevated a "struggle . . . entered solely to protect U.S. neutral rights into a 'war to end war,' a war for a democratic world order"[5] that dedicated, for the duration, what had been a blind power struggle. His famous Fourteen Points undoubtedly hastened Germany's surrender. Nevertheless, in his self-destroying zeal to further high moral

[3] *The War with Germany, A Statistical Summary*, Leonard P. Ayres, Government Printing Office, 1919.

[4] *Limited War*, Robert E. Osgood, University of Chicago Press, 1957, p. 92.

[5] Ibid., p. 92.

principles after the conflict, no less than in his prewar behavior, President Wilson was utterly unable to grasp the military factors upon which his policies would ultimately stand or fall. To varying degrees, such blindness has appeared as a curious characteristic of so many American leaders. Our history might have been written quite differently had not Washington and Lincoln been outstanding exceptions.[6]

The great lesson of World War I, for the United States, was the discovery of "industrial mobilization" (later to give way to the more inclusive term "economic mobilization") and its vital impact upon war in the first half of the twentieth century. Some salient features in that lesson are highly relevant to our concern with the impact of technology upon U.S. military policy. Largely because of it, and the cushion of time afforded by Britain's dogged defense, this country became the "arsenal of democracy" in World War II. Painfully learned in one war, masterfully applied in a later one, the lesson of economic mobilization finally led us astray for a time in the nuclear age when only ready forces tend to count.

The Industrialization of Wars

It can be said of all combatants in World War I that they were ill-prepared for the type of conflict which they set in motion. None of them foresaw the long drawn-out battle of attrition and the insatiable demands for all types of munitions which became the salient characteristics of the protracted struggle. Neither the military leaders nor their civilian

[6] *The Military Genius of Abraham Lincoln*, Brigadier General Colin R. Ballard, World Publishing Co., 1952.

chiefs of state anticipated the necessity for mobilizing all the resources of the nation, not merely the huge conscript armies. Leaders everywhere were guilty, to a greater or lesser extent, of what British Prime Minister David Lloyd George described as "mental obtuseness in failing to keep abreast of the modern developments and patterns in munitions and in machinery for munitions production." Industrial strength had unexpectedly emerged as the new measure of power, just as the problem of equipping armies exceeded those of recruiting and training them.

Long before the fighting ceased it was obvious that at the base of the struggle was a contest between chemists, scientists, and manufacturers. Numerous technological advances affected the character of the First World War; techniques of precision manufacturing and mass production probably foremost among them. Military applications of the internal combustion engine resulted in the tanks and airplanes that came to dominate tactics; the trucks that refashioned combat zone logistics and sometimes provided the means for decisive troop movements. Weapon complexity and the ever increasing range and weight of fire power made it more and more certain that future major conflicts could take place only between highly industrialized nations.

Interrelationships between military and civilian affairs appeared everywhere. Military planners provided specifications, schedules, and quantities to the civilian manufacturers. The competing demands of the civilian and military economies were reconciled by a new breed of statesmen, such as Newton D. Baker and Bernard Baruch, compelled to learn the business side of war in order to direct the conflict.

A late-comer in the conflict, the U.S. might have profited from the painful and costly lessons of our allies. But our long obsession with staying out of the war rendered our government unperceptive to the phenomena of the conflict. The United States had fewer military observers in Europe than had been sent to Manchuria over a decade previously to study the Russo-Japanese War. Travel by U.S. citizens in the "war zone" was sternly discouraged. No agency of our government displayed any interest in studying the unprecedented industrial upheavals occurring in England, France, and Germany. Press photographs of women working in munitions factories; of ammunition dumps, each containing more artillery shells than the U. S. Army's entire stock,—these were curiosities. Newspaper stories of Germany's "ersatz" substitutes for familiar articles of daily use passed for jokes.

Only one lesson of the war in Europe was learned in time, the military draft. The skeleton General Staff, having studied Britain's experience, had quietly prepared the basic study that later became the Selective Service Act on May 18, 1917. This prescience proved vital because after the administration severed diplomatic relations with Germany on February 3, General Staff work on a conscription bill was forbidden by the White House. Fortunately the work, already accomplished, could be made available a few weeks later when Wilson again reversed himself.

The planning of procurement policies for matériel to complement the Staff's manpower program received much less attention. The General Staff of 1916–17 lacked adequate coordinating contact with and authority over the Army's independent supply bureaus (Quartermaster, Ordnance, etc.).

Neither the U. S. Government nor the public appreciated until too late the extent of the industrial problems invoked by World War I although evidence was readily available in Europe. The 1916 Defense Act had empowered the President to seize industries which failed to comply with orders for war materials. Few realized that this provision could remedy only a difficulty which proved extremely rare, a recalcitrant industry. It could in no way improve the situation soon to confront the nation, industry's utter incapacity to rapidly convert production from scheduled peacetime items to the unfamiliar munitions now demanded at accelerated schedules.

The business and labor leaders comprising the Advisory Commission of the Council of National Defense took the initiative by February 1917, trying to calculate matériel requirements for a million-man army.[7] A few days later the War College Division of the General Staff ordered the Army's supply bureaus to estimate both amounts of matériel and time necessary to equip a like force.[8] The coincidence may well have been influenced through the Advisory Commission's contacts with Secretary of War Baker.

Yet slow as they were to grasp the problem, the military was first in the country to appreciate its enormity. In March 1917, Brigadier General William Crozier, Army Chief of Ordnance, estimated it would take two and a half years to provide a million-man army with artillery, eighteen months to outfit it with ammunition and machine guns. The Medical Corps Chief, Major General William C. Gorgas, set eight to twelve months for procurement of medical equipment. Major General George O. Squier, the Chief Signal Officer, expected to achieve the goal of his branch in six months, but foresaw a year to outfit the programed twenty squadrons of the "Aviation Section."

[7] *Industrial America in the World War*, Grosvenor B. Clarkson, Houghton Mifflin Co., 1923, p. 30.

[8] *History of Military Mobilization in the U. S. Army*, Kreidberg and Henry, Department of the Army Pamphlet, 20–212, 1955, p. 230.

A War Secretary's "Criminal" Actions

All estimates began with the yet unknown date upon which Congress would make funds available. On February 22, the House passed the normal $250,000,000 Army appropriations bill, unaltered by the recent trend of events. Even after the U.S. had entered the war, Newton D. Baker felt compelled to take upon himself the responsibility for obligating funds not yet appropriated by Congress while "scrupulously refraining from the least criticism"[9] of that body.

With Congress appalled at the Army's request for $3,000,000,000 Baker had only $30,000,000, the War Department's share of an emergency fund placed at the President's disposal. For ten weeks, until Congress passed another Appropriation Bill on June 15, the Secretary of War deliberately and repeatedly violated criminal statutes to initiate the vast flow of supplies essential to the expanding Army.

In those pre-budget system days every *item* had to be presented for Congressional approval before purchase. Baker never omitted an item nor the explanation as to those already ordered. The War Secretary won Congress' support and retained it although compelled to defend his policies before a Senate investigating committee in December which considered creating a Department of Munitions to take over military procurement.

Under the stress of the war's beginning the principal con-

[9] *The Impact of War*, Pendleton Herring, Farrar and Rinehart, New York, 1941, p. 89.

structive proposal came from Major General Leonard Wood who urged adoption of British and French weapons to save time. Opposition by General Crozier and the General Staff (May 1917) prevented official acceptance. Crozier averred that: "dependence upon another nation for our arms and ammunition is contrary to the independent spirit of our people . . ."[10] The fact remained that our Army at least would be dependent upon Allied equipment with which to fight.

The 1st Division sailed for France in June without steel helmets, which it later obtained from the British Army. The same month orders for 1,000,000 improved Enfield (British) rifles were issued to two U.S. firms which had been making the inferior model for the British (Remington and Winchester Arms). The modification altered the Enfield's magazine, chamber, and bore to take the U.S. service ammunition (.30 rimless) instead of the British .303 rim cartridges. As early as July dire shortage of clothing, not merely of prescribed uniforms, seriously slowed the scheduled induction of draftees into the Army. In the months that followed, shortages appeared everywhere reaching into civilian supplies where mild attempts at rationing, notably sugar, were initiated. Much of the trouble arose from the inability to distribute what was actually available. Freight traffic tied itself into knots for miles outside Atlantic coast ports. Before the end of the year the President had seized all U.S. railroads to prevent a complete transportation breakdown.

The industrial side of American participation in World War I was not wholly black, however. In addition to the

10 *History of Mobilization in the U. S. Army,* Kreidberg and Henry, Department of the Army Pamphlet 20–212, 1955, p. 322.

remarkable achievement in producing cargo ships by assembly line methods the huge construction project of providing training camps went well. Troop housing at the war's start had a total capacity below 125,000, much of it in unusable locations. By the end of 1917 wholly new camps could house 1,500,000 men, despite political bickering over camp location and a last-minute change to 250-man companies instead of the 150-man strength upon which camp layout had been based. It is significant that the contracts for shipping and cantonments left minor details to the contractors and were not subjected to a continuous rain of change orders. In marked contrast, Army Ordnance continued to test machine guns and adopted "an entirely new type" in May 1917. Decision processes on combat aircraft design were chaotic and greatly delayed by repeated changes in relatively minor detail.

A footnote to training-camp problems was General Pershing's insistence upon putting the trainees in tent camps, according to Army tradition. He sailed for France unconvinced that the entire stock of commercial canvas in the country would not begin to meet the need. This incident typified the military's failure, save for a devoted, small minority, to understand industry's problems. Industrialists, intent upon business as usual, and busy with Allied orders, gave scant thought to the needs of the military with the exception of Bernard Baruch and the few approaching his stature. As for the government, Congress apparently believed that authorizing the President to seize recalcitrant factories sufficed and the Executive Branch, prior to March 1917, ignored the industrial side of war preparation to concentrate upon avoiding war itself.

Science in World War I

Nineteen months of U.S. participation in the First World War influenced American science out of proportion to the time interval. Vast, if disappointingly slow, efforts to equip this country's military establishment multiplied the size of existing research agencies and caused new ones to spring up throughout industry. This same compelling drive enforced lessons in the necessity for co-operative research on a large scale not merely among different industries, but in research that crossed disciplines to a remarkable extent for an era in which physicists held themselves aloof from chemists and mathematicians customarily ignored all other scientists.

Thus the marriage of scientific research and industry proceeded much further than its contemporaneous science-military liaison. The former produced a rapidly growing infant which was destined to remake the nation's way of life, at least outwardly, in a decade. The latter comprised a hasty union of which little survived upon the return to peace.

The circumstances of the science-military co-operation made an early parting inevitable. Scientists had offered their services to the Armed Services with the enthusiasm of a patriotic volunteer. They were welcomed like raw recruits. Scientists were commissioned and put into uniform, because the military's obsession with discipline could think of no other procedure. The views of scientist-volunteers were rarely asked. For example, an assignment as a mere major, Signal Officers' Reserve Corps, U. S. Army, was scarcely the most useful manner in which to employ the services of forty-nine-year-old Dr. Robert A. Millikan, a distinguished physicist, a member of the National Academy of Sciences and the Vice-Chairman of the National Research Council. It is true that the Navy placed Thomas A. Edison at the head of its Consulting Board but at the age of seventy the famous inventor was hardly the most suitable candidate for a reserve officer's commission.

The forming of the National Research Council in July 1916 had resulted more from the urgings of civilian scientists, than from the government. The Council's staff gathered in Washington upon the outbreak of war, after forming committees throughout the nation to represent all the principal fields of science. Characteristically, no government funds could be made immediately available. The Carnegie Corporation and the Rockefeller Foundation jointly financed the Council at the outset and continued to assist to the extent of matching all subsequent Federal allocations. By early 1918 the Council's offshoot, the Research Information Service, was belatedly seeking to learn what Allied research could tell this country.

A White House Executive Order creating a permanent National Research Council in May 1918 gave the Council official status shortly before the second anniversary of its founding. Responsibilities outlined in the order reflected lately acquired awareness of the necessity for active co-operation between civilian scientists and all branches of the government, civil and military. Regrettably, the wording suggested an *ad hoc* group for the emergency rather than an enduring national institution.

Whether or not President Wilson so intended, the Council's postwar policies justified the pessimistic forecast. A 1919 reorganization bestowed upon a Division of Governmental Relations all responsibility for contact with Federal agencies.

Council reports thereafter confirmed an attitude of aloofness from the government. "Meetings were few, plans nebulous and action not forthcoming."[11] Similar comment could doubtless be made of overtures to the Council from various Federal agencies.

The Reception of Scientist-Volunteers

While America waged war, however, the *rapprochement* between the military and the scientific community received the ungrudging support of both parties. The officers' uniforms worn by so many scientists were symbolic of two facts: distinguished leaders in their own fields had patriotically volunteered for the duration; their service was almost invariably under the orders of military professionals.

Instead of a partnership, a relationship of advisor and commanding officer prevailed. Certainly the majority of the advisors adjusted to unaccustomed procedures and much sound advice was duly heeded. But the period of effectiveness and harmony was short. With the advent of peace, the scientists ceased to concern themselves with military problems the moment they shed their uniforms. To regulars of the Army and Navy the entire matter seemed a wartime interlude, not permanent broadening of their profession.

Probably the smoothest working science-military team in World War I developed under Army Surgeon General Gorgas, famed for his conquest of disease during construction of the Panama Canal. In the field of medicine, "military necessity" and scientific goals required the minimum adjustment. Notable achievements resulted. Improved techniques

11 A. H. Dupree, *Science in the Federal Government*, p. 329.

cut death rates among the wounded. Servicemen's health was safeguarded better than that of civilians, even to protection against the epidemic of influenza. The medical score for the American Expeditionary Force stood 2.8 deaths in battle for each soldier dead from disease. While this does not equal the phenomenal rate of 5:1 achieved by the Japanese in Manchuria in 1905, only the virulent outbreak of "flu" in 1918 prevented American medical science from breaking that record. Nearly 83 per cent of all nonbattle deaths in the Army were attributed to influenza.[12]

The related science of psychiatry aided the military for the first time, at least in a deliberate role. Psychiatrists assisted in examination of drafted men and secured official acceptance of combat neuroses, popularly termed "shell shock," as a medical disability.

In the physical sciences weapons research was confronted with the urgent need for mass production. Improvements in existing models were restricted to those possible of attainment while industry set up assembly lines. Most research and development worthy of the name aimed at providing new weapons for combat employment no earlier than 1919–20. Among the notable developments maturing too late for battlefield use were the Liberty (airplane) motor, the Liberty truck, commercial production of helium for lighter-than-air craft, the battleships and battlecruisers of the short-lived "Navy Second to None" building program. The few exceptions, developments completed in time to influence the course of the war, included "triggers" for the North Sea mine barrage and underwater submarine detection gear.

The dilemma of early standardization versus improved

[12] *The War with Germany, A Statistical Summary,* Colonel Leonard P. Ayres, Government Printing Office, 1919, Chapter IX.

design increased with the complexity of the weapon, asserting itself most pointedly in the area of aircraft procurement. Lack of clear, compelling policy directives from the top levels of government and the military, kept scientists as well as industry in a state of confusion. The numerous failures to meet production schedules can seldom if ever be laid to the shortcomings of the scientists but rather to neglect of scientific advice in decision making.

Blind spots did of course mar the scientific effort so hastily mobilized and so rigidly regimented. The impetus in chemical warfare research had to come from General Pershing overseas, and even these efforts stumbled woefully behind immediate needs. Although gas warfare began April 1915 in Europe and a new chemical, "mustard gas," delivered in artillery shells, was reported in July 1917, it was September of that year before a "U. S. Gas Service" was constituted by Pershing in France after calling upon the War Department for equipment and personnel to investigate chemical warfare.[14]

Not infrequently scientific vision was frustrated for lack of time. Two agencies in America, the Navy and the Bureau of Mines, competed to build plants to produce helium for the hitherto unattainable fireproof dirigibles and balloons. The hydrogen-filled Zeppelins which had bombed London with impunity early in the war had suffered swift obsolescence when improved British fighter aircraft were equipped with incendiary bullets. However the Navy's program to build an Allied dirigible fleet went unrealized since the first shipments of commercial bulk helium did not reach dockside until November 1918.

[13] *My Experiences in the World War*, John J. Pershing, Frederic Stokes Company, Volume I, p. 167.

An American Army Is Born

The years 1917–18 transformed the U. S. Army from a token force into a first-rate military machine. In the process lessons were learned or overlooked, assimilated or forgotten because of chance, personalities, and American characteristics—but chiefly because that change was only temporary. By 1920 in fact, and by 1922 even on paper,[14] the U. S. Army was again incapable of supporting any important national policy, but it had ceased to be a mysterious, traditional symbol overly extolled in history books, condemned by labor leaders, and ignored by the vast majority of Americans. The Army had emerged from the war—and continued to provide— a nucleus, albeit of somewhat fluctuating value, for a potent force.

Far more important, the Army had intruded into the everyday life of millions of American families, each of which had definite opinions, right or mistaken, concerning it. Public disregard for the U. S. Army could no longer be attributed to honest ignorance, but only to the deliberate, if often subconscious, desire to avoid any further contact with "disagreeable" experience.

The 133,000-man Regular Army of April 1917 received 2,500,000 draftees for the "National Army" in the thirteen months ending October 1918 while its own ranks were being expanded four and one-half times. In addition, the National Guard increased sixfold from an original strength of 67,000. In startling contrast to all previous wars, much was accom-

[14] Congressional appropriations held the Army to half its legally authorized (280,000 men) strength.

plished on limited means. Regular officers were spread—necessarily very thinly—throughout all new units. The cadre system which provided newly organized regiments with a nucleus of trained commissioned and noncommissioned officers was adopted over Pershing's strenuous opposition.

In his urgent need for combat divisions, the A.E.F.'s commander naturally objected to a system which "stole men from combat divisions while they are completing their training.[15] Yet the General Staff's cadre system was an immense improvement over traditional procedures of raising new regiments inexperienced from colonel to private, previously forced upon the War Department by Congress. Also for the first time all officer appointments were made by the Federal Government not the states. Both of these changes were essential preparation for the losses anticipated in the war of attrition being fought in France.

In actual combat also the U. S. Army demonstrated a keener awareness than its experienced French and British allies of the kind of tactics which an industrial war permitted. Evidence of a major departure in German tactics, away from trench warfare's indecisive blood baths toward open, fluid attack, came with the news of enemy victories at Riga and Caporetto in late 1917. In these battles the Germans relied upon infiltration and surprise instead of the prolonged artillery preparation and costly mass attacks which had characterized their tactics for the three previous years. Despite this evidence, French instructors as late as 1918 harshly condemned American insistence upon training combat units for open warfare in addition to the customary indoctrination in trench fighting. But General Pershing was adamant about

15 *My Experiences in the World War*, John J. Pershing, Volume I, p. 380.

going his own way. Beginning with his service on the Mexican border, "Black Jack" held his staff strictly to the line that a war of movement was the principal objective. Trench warfare he regarded as a temporary phase to be mastered only as a means to the greater end.

Thus it was no accident that the first real breakthrough of German lines on the Western Front was achieved by Pershing's divisions, assembled for the first time into an American Army, at Saint-Mihiel on September 12–16, 1918. The maximum advance was only sixteen miles, on a twenty-five-mile front, but in four years' fighting, Allied progress had usually been measured in yards. Even more shocking to Anglo-French conservatives, in this thrust the losses of the German defenders, in prisoners alone, exceeded twice the total casualties of the attackers. Pershing reported that "Without doubt an immediate continuation of the advance would have carried us well beyond the Hindenburg line, possibly into Metz."[16] However the impending, greater offensive in the Meuse-Argonne prevented the attempt.

A major innovation at Saint-Mihiel was the employment of air power, massed principally for ground attack though reinforced by the British Independent Bombing Squadron which struck German railheads behind the salient. The group of nearly 1400 planes, under Colonel William Mitchell, was the strongest aviation force assembled up to that time. The Germans had initiated concentrated, direct air support in their March 1918 offensive, using 300 aircraft. Yet this display of American combat organization and prowess owed nothing to American technology. Very few of the aircraft, none of the 3000 pieces of artillery, and not one

[16] *My Experiences in the World War*, John J. Pershing, Volume II, p. 270.

of the three hundred tanks came from U.S. production lines although U.S. troops manned most of them. The hundreds of trucks that furnished logistic support came from French factories.

When the Saint-Mihiel operation was followed with unprecedented speed by the larger Meuse-Argonne attack, American soldiers irrefutably demonstrated their proficiency to many doubters, both friend and foe. On September 26, only ten days after the Saint-Mihiel drive, almost 600,000 men had been moved "by the left flank" from one area to the other and smoothly replaced the 200,000 French defenders of the Argonne lines. The movements were worked out under the able direction of Colonel George C. Marshall, Jr., of the General Staff, First Army.[17]

The U. S. Army's operational achievements bespoke a new excellence in a field which previously had all but been ignored, namely logistics. General Pershing's successful struggle to form an American Army despite French and British pressure to employ our troops as riflemen and machine gunner replacements in their own formations—and his wisdom in preparing for a campaign of maneuver—showed no greater leadership than the acumen with which he founded a firm logistic base for the A.E.F.'s operations. The difficulties overcome were undeniably greatest in the last of these tasks.

Statistics of construction accomplished in France—from lumberjacking in jealously guarded French forests to building and equipping railroads, highways, camps, and depots plus establishing ports at small fishing villages—read like the miracles they were to European eyes. Army Engineers took

[17] *My Experiences in the World War*, John J. Pershing, Volume II, p. 285.

over construction from the Quartermaster who had bureau-
cratically guarded that prerogative through the years and
still retained it in the United States.[18] Railroads and later
motor transportation were set up as new military services.[19]
Perhaps the most startling index of this new emphasis, to
military men at least, was Pershing's assignment of his best
combat commander, Major General James C. Harbord,
("the finest soldier in the U. S. Army" Pershing's enco-
mium) to command the Services of Supply.[20] Harbord took
up his logistic duties fresh from battlefield triumphs at
Château-Thierry where he commanded the 2nd Division.

A.E.F. Creates a Viable General Staff

In the realm of staff organization, the A.E.F. also built
lastingly, from the ground up. Pershing's opinion of the War
Department General Staff was characteristically blunt: "Not
yet properly organized . . . prominent bureau chiefs, dis-
bursing government funds, continuously opposed development of this planning and co-ordinating agency superior to

[18] Chief of Staff George C. Marshall invoked the precedent of his old
commander on the eve of World War II, and extended it to the United
States. This time Congress did not reverse the military's action after hostilities. Construction remains an Engineer responsibility today.

[19] This essential organization change also had to be repeated at the onset
of World War II. Congress abolished the Transportation Corps in 1920
reassigning its functions to the overloaded Quartermaster Corps.

[20] This appointment, July 28, 1918, closely followed Secretary Baker's
suggestion that Major General Goethals leave his War Department General
Staff post to head the S.O.S. in France in a "co-ordinate rather than a subordinate position" to Pershing. The suggestion, firmly rejected by the A.E.F.
commander as a violation of "unity of command," was the culmination of
a series of differences between Pershing and the Washington Chief of Staff,
General Peyton C. March. (My Experiences in the World War, John J.
Pershing, Vol. II, p. 185–86.)

them."[21] Pershing made the development of a satisfactory General Staff system to meet the demands of modern warfare a high priority task of the A.E.F. Opposition to the original General Staff in Congress and within the Army itself, especially in the entrenched Washington bureaus, had handicapped its development as planned by Elihu Root. Worst of all, in Pershing's opinion, was the "lack of a clear conception of the Staff's proper functions and the erroneous centralization of mere details"[22] in the hands of the Chief of Staff. These weaknesses the A.E.F. commander proceeded to eliminate while retaining the true strengths of the General Staff system.

Drawing upon the experience of the U. S. Army and, according to Pershing, selecting the best features of the French and British staff systems, the A.E.F. organized a General Staff to lead rather than follow the one in the War Department. The A.E.F. General Staff became, by 1920, the basic model for all U. S. Army staffs to the present time. Its four principal divisions were G-1 Administration, G-2 Intelligence, G-3 Operations and Training, and G-4 Coordination. Later Pershing added a fifth section, G-5 Training, to correct deficiencies in the Stateside instruction of troops sent to him, but his most drastic changes had to do with the logistical side of war, so long the Achilles heel of American armies.

Of the eight new branches of the Army that Pershing found it necessary to create, only two, the Tank Corps and Aviation, were primarily designed for combat and one, the Chemical Service, partially so. The others, Forestry Service,

[21] Ibid., Vol. I, p. 17.

[22] Ibid., p. 103.

Railroad Transport, Motor Transport, Military Police, and Construction were distinctly noncombatant services without which the combat arms could not function effectively. That all these new elements were created in the A.E.F.[23] and most of them abolished in Washington after the war, only to be revived twenty years later, is significant of the difference between an independent theater commander's viewpoint and the politically charged atmosphere in which the War Department had to function.

These new establishments were efficiently integrated with the older ones in the A.E.F. to obtain a teamwork between combat and logistic elements that in some respects excelled that of many overseas theaters in which U.S. troops have fought since. A single example indicates the trend. Pershing overruled an appointed board of officers' opinion that centralized purchasing was illegal and established a Purchasing Board with representatives of each Service, plus the Red Cross and the Y.M.C.A., to control all A.E.F. buying. Lieutenant Colonel (later Brigadier General and future Vice-President) Charles Gates Dawes, 17th Engineers, "a man of large business experience" was put in charge of the Board. The Board, "in a Europe supposedly stripped of supplies, gathered some ten million tons of military material for the American Army compared to some seven million tons sent over from the U.S."[24]

Much later, under the stress of dire military danger in June 1918, the French and British, who had long sought to use U.S. manpower in a common pool from which to draw

[23] Pershing, en route to France, decided to separate Aviation from the Signal Corps, contrary to War Department policy. *American Army in France*, James G. Harbord, Little Brown, 1936, p. 75.

[24] Ibid., p. 127.

their combat units, were finally persuaded to permit unified use of logistic facilities. These pioneering procurement and fiscal procedures of the A.E.F. reduced the strain on over-seas shipping by utilizing European raw materials as well as end items. Their principles were extensively followed by U.S. forces, some two decades later, in World War II in the famed "reverse lend-lease" programs.

Military Management

Unfortunately, the Washington command post, by 1918 a confusing mixture of General Staff and civilian manage-ment, never attained the operating efficiency of A.E.F. head-quarters. The reasons for this unfavorable comparison partially excuse the deficiencies along the Potomac. Over-all management of the war effort hugely exceeded the magnitude of an overseas theater's tasks. Greater urgency confronted the national headquarters. No element of the military machinery could begin to function until Washington decided, ordered, produced and delivered. This applied equally to decisions directed toward training programs, combat operations, or supply support of either. There was no time, in the midst of this pressure, to plan wisely and organize well, as the A.E.F. could do during 1917 because only a trickle of resources and men reached France; only five divisions and 350,000 tons of supplies by January 1918. Washington carried the burden of allaying public and Congressional clamor for action while simultaneously expanding the war effort manyfold despite repeated radical changes in the goals of that effort.

Not least among the last named difficulties were those imposed by General Pershing himself, who demanded major alterations in everything from force levels to specific items of equipment. The first major change came with the A.E.F.'s decision to create oversize divisions instead of the approximately 12,000 strength recommended by the War Department General Staff and current in European armies. Pershing's figure for his division was 27,000 combat troops. Addition of service support brought the total to 40,000, the number employed by Staff planners for the remainder of the war.[25]

Secretary Baker approved the Pershing division in line with his policy of giving the A.E.F. commander complete operational authority. This disrupted not only the cantonment program but involved completely reworking all tables of organization and equipment, personnel allocation, and school programs of instruction. This was no minor setback for an overworked General Staff desperately trying to expand twentyfold with wholly inexperienced newcomers.

Pershing Clashes with March

As months passed military requirements multiplied beyond the capabilities of even a reorganized War Department and the mobilizing nation. Under Baker's policy, General Pershing's recommendations still generally carried the weight of "orders" to the General Staff in Washington. However, in midsummer of 1918, the new Chief of Staff, General Peyton Conway March, balked when Pershing sought a 100 division force instead of the 80 decided upon that spring.

[25] This is the first known enunciation of the concept of the "division slice," a figure obtained by dividing Army strength by the number of combat divisions in the Army; a logistics planning device widely used in World War II.

This time the Secretary of War backed his own staff. Further increase, he ruled, was impossible.

Pershing complained to Baker of "poor direction of the war effort in the War Department" but the Secretary withheld knowledge of the letter from General March who, in turn, charged Pershing with "inability to function in teamwork with his legal and authorized superiors." Quite aside from personalities involved (Pershing had in fact recommended March, an A.E.F. brigadier general of artillery, for his exalted post) the dispute arose inevitably from the uncertainties in U. S. Army organization. Was the War Department Chief of Staff commanding general of the Army or was he, as Pershing felt, really subordinate to the field commander?

As recently as July 1916, Judge Advocate General Enoch H. Crowder had sent Baker a memorandum stringently restricting General Staff authority on legal grounds under the National Defense Act of Juy 1916. Two months later, in the Elihu Root tradition, Secretary Baker rejected Crowder's advice and bluntly reaffirmed the authority of the Chief of Staff, then Major General Hugh L. Scott, over all bureaus and agencies of the War Department. But that had been only another "bureau chiefs' revolts." There was no precedent for dealing with an overseas Theater Commander whose forces consumed all the military resources the nation could send him and then negotiated directly with the Allies for more.

In an effort to resolve the difficulties without losing the highly valuable services of either Pershing or March, Secretary Baker accepted the latter's suggestion that General Goethals, assistant chief of the War Department General Staff and Director of Purchase Storage and Traffic, be placed in charge of all Army supplies from their origin in the U.S. to the combat zone in France. Ostensibly designed to "relieve" Pershing from concern over his ports and Line of Communications, the move was a thinly veiled restriction of his authority. As noted, Pershing's blunt refusal of the Secretary's "suggestion" kept General Goethals in the U.S. Instead, General Harbord, Pershing's appointee and subordinate, commanded the Services of Supply, new title for the Line of Communications in France, for the rest of the war.

Shortcomings of the Washington Command Post

It would be unfair and absurd to blame A.E.F. intransigence for all the shortcomings of the Washington command post. The major causes of failure were faulty organization, wholly inadequate strength, and lack of foresighted planning, possibly in that order. Considering the last one, Benedict Crowell, Assistant Secretary of War, indicted the General Staff of "ignorance of the business of supplying a modern army," pointing out that when the newly created General Munitions Board sought General Staff studies on supply problems it "received only a few pamphlets of no practical value." Similarly it was not until February 1918 that the General Staff appointed Leonard P. Ayres, a recently commissioned investment counsel, to establish a Statistics Branch although it had long been the Staff's responsibility to collect, collate, and evaluate military information. The discovery that wartime operations could not be efficiently controlled without professional organization of such data had been late and costly.

In fairness, the problems of industrial mobilization as it

came to be termed were only partially solvable by the General Staff. Crowell himself was among a strong and vocal group which held that wartime production and distribution of supplies should be handled by civilians, not the military whose function would be to state military requirements only. Both the Army and Navy opposed this procedure, suspecting that their needs might not be met by civilian procurement agencies. This debate, altered only in form, stands unresolved today.

Legal restrictions on the size of the General Staff, made more stringent in the 1916 Defense Act although that law expanded the Army at least on paper, accounted for fault number two, inadequate strength. By November 1918 the War Department General Staff had grown until the office of the Chief of Staff (to co-ordinate the co-ordinators) alone had 51 officers and 80 civilians assigned, considerably more than the total on duty with the General Staff nineteen months earlier. That the Staff had been unable to foresee and plan for major expansion in emergency is not so easily excused.

As for faulty organization, that condition had been—and continued to be—chronic. The War Department, as prophesied by General Johnson Hagood[26] in 1926, was again compelled to reorganize dramatically on the eve of World War II. In 1917, the flaws were even more obvious. According to General March's later report,[27] five different agencies were responsible for storage and issue of supplies, ten separately handled finances, nine distinct methods were in use for estimating requirements. As Assistant Secretary Crowell com-

[26] *Services of Supply*, Johnson Hagood, Houghton Mifflin, Co., 1927.

[27] Report of the Chief of Staff, U. S. Army, 1919.

plained, it was as if a "huge factory tried to run itself without overhead direction, and control."

A costly example had appeared early in the war when the French government startled Washington with a demand for 45,000 U.S. aviators and a correspondingly great amount of aviation matériel to be delivered in France within the year. At the time no U.S. aviation industry existed. There were scarcely one hundred qualified pilots in the country. Nevertheless under the urging of public enthusiasm a program was adopted and undertaken by the Signal Corps. The program was implemented practically independently and was clearly disproportionate to a properly balanced Army. As should have been foreseen it proved impossible of execution. The two billion dollar failure already noted was the result.

Reorganization of the War Department

By December 1917 the lack of co-ordination in the War Department presaged collapse of the nation's military program. A hostile Congress and popular clamor, no longer enthusiastic, compelled reorganization. The new setup, effective February 1918, was only mildly revised after General March became Chief of Staff the following month for the duration. Five staff sections emerged: Executive, War Plans, Operations, Intelligence, and Purchase-Storage and Traffic.

The biggest innovation came in the Purchase-Storage and Traffic Section boldly created for General Goethals whose reputation as a skilled organizer had been established when he built the Panama Canal. The Army's five original supply bureaus were left with procurement on technical items but, in the United States, Purchase-Storage and Traffic (almost to the extent the title indicates) were finally placed under a single director.[28] Contrary to the Chief of Staff's desires, but in deference to Pershing's insistence, overseas logistics remained under the theater commander's authority.

Although Army management of procurement, the business aspects of war, caused internal War Department turmoil and violent criticism from civilian agencies of the Federal Government, there was no important cleavage over strategy. Once war had been declared, the President and Congress left the conduct of combat operations in the hands of the Secretaries of the two military departments, who in turn exercised their authority in unequivocal support of their selected overseas commanders, General John J. Pershing and Admiral William S. Sims. This fortunate situation, for the military, was at variance with that which had prevailed in the war with Spain. It also differed markedly from conditions in England and France.

In England, Prime Minister Lloyd George's bitter row with Field Marshal Haig and the Chief of the Imperial General Staff undoubtedly contributed to the success of the German offensives in the spring of 1918. In France, Georges Clemenceau's highly quotable growl that "war is too serious a business to be left to generals" suggests the nature of affairs once "The Tiger" became Premier. A possible explanation for the contrast may lie in the fact that World War I reached the American people only via military logistics; supply, transportation and accommodations for troops. Casualties were relatively light. America's national safety was never di-

[28] Dismemberment of this office came swiftly after the war only to be, in principle, restored with even more extensive powers under General Brehon B. Somervell, Commanding Army Service Forces in 1942. Army Service Forces, in turn, did not long survive World War II.

rectly threatened. Quite the reverse was the case for Britain and France.

In this country, a closing footnote on Army management and command structure discloses a notable superiority over that of the Navy, still firmly in the grasp of independent Bureau Chiefs. The recently established office of Chief of Naval Operations possessed only very modest powers. Yet, paradoxically, it was chiefly the Navy that displayed military technologies worthy of the nation it defended. Ranking in over-all sea power behind the navies of only Britain and Germany, the U. S. Navy had oil-burning capital ships in her battle line that equaled—and some authorities insisted they surpassed—any afloat. Mechanical computers assisted an excellent gunnery control, Navy radio was the best. According to some authorities[29] these achievements proceeded less from scientific research on the part of the Navy Department than borrowings from abroad, especially from the British. Cruiser strength was deficient however and submarines, early developed in the U.S., utterly neglected.

Naval Operations

The difference in combat readiness and technological status of the Navy, compared to the Army, resulted in wholly dissimilar responses and roles for the two services. As might have been expected of a "first line of defense," U.S. naval strength made itself felt in the war long before the Army could commit any troops to combat. The destroyer force of the Atlantic Fleet had a division of six destroyers in Queens-

[29] *Science in the Federal Government*, A. H. Dupree, Harvard University Press, 1957, p. 304.

town, Ireland, four weeks after war was declared. These vessels were immediately ordered into the critical antisubmarine campaign by an admiral of the Royal Navy with full approval of Admiral Sims, commander of all U. S. Naval Forces in European waters. Sims reached London on April 9 by Navy Department orders. General Pershing arrived in France on June 13.

Army units first joined their Allies in the trenches November 3. In contrast thirty-four U.S. destroyers, effectively supported by repair and supply ships, comprised within sixty days almost the total strength of Queenstown, the important British forward base in the battle of the Atlantic. A division of five coal-burning U.S. battleships had simultaneously joined the Grand Fleet at Scapa Flow, even to the extent of employing Royal Navy signals and tactics, to further insure that armada's superiority over the German High Seas Fleet. An acute shortage of fuel oil in the British Isles made the more modern U.S. warships logistic white elephants. Coal was relatively plentiful from British sources.

Under a policy diametrically opposed to that of Pershing, Sims decided to use U.S. naval forces as reinforcements to the Allied Navies.[30] Both leaders received wholehearted backing from their respective civilian chiefs back home and, if history "proves" anything, results justified their persistence in the face of severe criticism. Pershing's stand was attacked by Allied leaders who hoped to use American manpower as fillers in their own depleted divisions, while Sims' "teamwork" roused the ire of large segments of the American public still fundamentally hostile to England.

[30] *The Victory at Sea*, W. S. Sims, John Murray, London, 1920, p. 36.

The Navy Joins the War Against U-Boats

Radically different situations confronted the U. S. Army and Navy in the early summer of 1917. In France the Allied armies' costly offensives had not yet been recognized as the suicidal failures they actually were but at sea the stepped up U-boat assault on Allied shipping seriously endangered the very life of Britain. For the first time in a century Britain, although still undisputed mistress of the world's broad oceans, had lost control of the sea approaches to the British Isles. Submarine technology had radically expanded the meaning of sea power. Supremacy on the high seas now necessitated means, as yet undeveloped, to control not only the surface but the waters beneath. A second expansion, mastery of the air space above the waters, would be one of technology's impacts on a later, greater, war.

Conservative and highly secret British estimates set as the fall of 1917 the date on which England would be unable to continue hostilities if shipping losses were not drastically lowered. Sims, working intimately with the British Admiralty, recognized the urgency—and the solution. There was no time to spare for establishing U.S. bases, headquarters, and supporting shore establishments from which a "U.S. fleet" could operate. Destroyer protection which had prevented German submarines from sinking a single British battleship must be given to merchant shipping. This meant a return to traditional convoying of fleets of merchantmen, a tactic employed against sea raiders for centuries.

There were two major difficulties:[31] a desperate shortage

[31] Sims, Op. Cit., p. 89.

of destroyers, before the entry of the U.S. into the war, and a deep mistrust of merchant marine seamanship. Merchant-ship masters themselves insisted that the multi-ship maneuvers involved in zigzagging a large convoy would sink more ships from collision than U-boats could destroy. U.S. reinforcements, added as fast as they could be made available to the naval resources of the Royal Navy, gradually overcame the first obstacle. An astonishingly successful, experimental convoy, from the Mediterranean to England in late May 1917, won over the skeptical merchant mariners.

On May 21, the Admiralty officially adopted the convoy system. Results were almost immediately apparent. Ship losses never again reached the appalling total of 875,000 tons sunk in April 1917. After October they dropped, and stayed, below 400,000 tons per month, the 1917–18 average. As early as July, Sims had cabled the Navy Department that "the convoy system will beat the submarine menace," explaining that management of ocean convoys resembled the handling of freight cars on the U.S. railways; "gateways" were established for their assembly; cruisers or battleships guarded them against surface commerce raiders on the high seas; meticulously timed destroyer escorts took over as the submarine zones were reached. The World War I U-boat, unlike its 1942 descendants, was restricted in range. Publicized transatlantic voyages of the cargo submarine *Deutschland* and the combat U-53 were stunts not serious threats. Actually the first, one-way, ocean crossing of the Atlantic by submarines was achieved by ten undersea craft built by Bethlehem Steel, assembled in Canada and manned by British crews.

The antisubmarine campaign rapidly expanded with American participation. A U.S. contingent of 41 ships at Britain's Gibraltar station included Coast Guard cutters, converted yachts, even five ancient destroyers from Manila, 420 tonners in a day of 1200 ton ships of that type. The sub-chaser, a tiny ship designed to fight U-boats in coastal waters, began as an 80-footer built in U.S. yards for the Allies and shipped across the Atlantic as "deck loads." The U. S. Navy redesigned these craft at 110 feet, ordered 400 from contractors and sailed nearly half as many to Europe during the winter gales of 1917–18.

Stationed in three divisions—at Queenstown for Irish sea patrols, Plymouth for work in the English Channel, Corfu for Adriatic duty—these small ships reduced the strain on destroyers. When large convoys neared their destination the practice was to break into detachments, each of which proceeded to their own port of destination. For this last leg of the journey—and for the short runs incident to collecting outbound convoys—the small subchasers took responsibility. They were also the first ships to employ underwater listening devices to seek out U-boats.

Three U.S. corporations had undertaken work on submarine detection gear before 1917; working on the principle of the underwater bell which warned liners of shoal areas in foggy weather. When the U.S. entered the war a co-ordinating board in the Navy Department, co-operating with Allied scientists, pushed the project to operational tests by the fall of 1917.

The subchasers' "C-tube," a rubber-tipped iron pipe lowered into the sea and wired to earphones, was fairly effective for azimuth but not for range. Three "chasers" floating in line—the device was drowned out by the parent ship's own engines when under way—sought a "fix" on a submarine by triangulation then, at high speed, dashed to the located point to discharge depth bombs.

Unexpected help also came from Allied submarines. Results achieved by these boats on antisub patrols disproved the prevalent theory that submarines could not fight submarines. Scouting at periscope depth to spot U-boats sailing on the surface to recharge their short-lived batteries, Allied undersea craft scored, on a ship for ship basis, five times as many kills as destroyers in the last year of the war.

The World's Biggest Mine Field

Another major technological achievement of the U. S. Navy, a mine barrage to blockade the North Sea from Scotland to Norway, began in 1917. No undertaking of such scope had ever been contemplated in naval operations. To block 250 miles of sea, averaging 600 feet in depth, some 400,000 mines were called for, considerably more than the world stockage. For existing U. S. Navy and Royal Navy mines of the contact type to be effective against submarines, multiple layers in depth had to be placed.

In this dilemma, the U. S. Navy drew upon a prototype firing device for a submarine gun invented by Ralph C. Browne, an electrical engineer of Salem, Massachusetts, and redesigned by the Bureau of Ordnance in August 1917. Two months' experimentation converted this ingenious but comparatively uesless invention into a reliable mine "trigger" that enabled one mine to do the work of four in the North Sea barrier. A small buoy supported a long, thin copper cable or antenna attached to the mine below. Any U-boat making contact with the cable detonated the mine beneath and was destroyed.

This apparently minor technological "breakthrough" encouraged the U.S. and British governments to jointly adopt the barrier project on November 2, 1917. Production of the mines was rushed. In May 1918 a special U.S. mine-laying squadron arrived in Scotland and began placement, assisted by a smaller British flotilla. The barrage was over 75 per cent in place when Germany surrendered and work was discontinued. While actual losses inflicted on enemy submarines by the mine field could not be determined it was doubtless the major contributor to the list of U-boats recorded as "missing at sea." In addition, damage to the morale of German submarine crews was appreciable, contributing to their revolt late in the war.

In addition to experiencing antisubmarine warfare for the first time, the Navy encountered the unfamiliar problems of naval aviation which expanded proportionately more than any other part of the Navy. Unlike the Army, the Navy set about manufacturing its own combat aircraft with better results than its sister service realized from industry. In July 1917, Secretary Josephus Daniels ordered a naval aircraft factory established at Philadelphia. Work began on the plant's first flying boat only sixty-seven days later. By June 1918, ten months from the Secretary's order, one H-16 flying boat of U.S. design was completed each day. By late summer the installation converted to an assembly line for contractor's components, shifting to the F-5-L a British aircraft powered by the U. S. Liberty motor. Construction by the Navy of an airplane factory at Pauillac, France, scheduled for large-scale production in the spring of 1919, was unfinished at the war's end.

U. S. Naval aviators were flying combat sorties from British and French bases in Europe by June 1917, using Allied planes. The first detachment, seven pilots and 122 mechanics, commanded by a Lieutenant Whiting, operated out of Dunkirk. In contrast to the tight control General Pershing maintained over all activities of the A.E.F., Admiral Sims learned about Whiting's activities from the British Admiralty. Sims' reaction was praise for Whiting's initiative. A naval "Northern Bombing Group" staged some attacks on German submarine bases in Belgium but available records make more mention of an Army-Navy controversy over possession of the then prized Italian Caproni bombers than on-target damage resulting from their strikes.

Another evidence of Navy initiative that won Sims' praise, this time on land, was the counter to German long range artillery in France. Five 14-inch naval guns,[32] mounted on specially built railroad cars arrived in France in July 1918. Army Engineers contrived to get them over French rail lines designed for no such loads and the guns went into action at the unusual range—for mobile cannon—of 18–23 miles.

Throughout the war the Navy sought to expedite construction of its program for the world's most powerful battle fleet. The 1916 program for 50 destroyers received top priority and multiplied sixfold, almost 300 warships of this type being completed before the end of 1918. Simultaneously work on twelve "post-Jutland superdreadnought" battleships and half as many battle cruisers, each technologically superior to any afloat, was begun. Of these only the three 16-inch gun battleships of the *Maryland* class and two battlecruisers, completed as aircraft carriers, were ever commissioned. Postwar economies put a damper on "big Navy" adherents in Congress. The 1922 Naval Disarmament Treaty applied the *coup de grâce*.

[32] Sims, Op. Cit., Pershing, Vol. I, p. 107, states twenty-four 8-inch mortars and *six* 14-inch naval guns were the only U.S. manufactured artillery pieces used in combat.

Forgotten Lessons

It is obvious that the many applications of technology to World War I prior to our actual involvement in that conflict had negligible impact upon U.S. foreign or military policy. Once we joined the belligerent ranks, the requirements of military technologies had an all-pervasive influence upon the scope and frenzied haste of our industrial mobilization. In the realm of weaponry, that mobilization's contribution to the American Expeditionary Force in France was pitifully insufficient though it did materially aid the vital antisubmarine campaign.

As had been the case in 1898, our Navy required far less expansion and battle priming than the Army to become capable of a significant combat effort. Unlike our Spanish-American War experience, however, the U. S. Army of 1917 was technologically, not merely quantitatively, inferior to that of other nations. In preparation for land warfare the United States had lost ground during the two decades of rapid scientific-technical military progress.

With all the dedication in the world, American scientists could give only marginal assistance to weapons improvements in the brief time available. Successful scientific collaboration in military research programs demanded, even forty years ago, a longer period for fruition than the fourteen months prior to the June 1918 battlefield crisis in Europe.

Efforts to provide scientific management for the military by means of the General Staff and industrial mobilization, demanded by the new technological predominance in warfare, promised a full measure of success by 1919. The earlier termination of the conflict was due in large measure to America's brilliant military leadership and politico-strategic policy direction.

The United States had, involuntarily, emerged from the war in the foremost rank of world powers only to withdraw into isolation. The vital lessons learned would be quickly forgotten, belatedly to be recalled for use in a greater war. The proposed strategies of the military, their organization and combat strength in being, the reserves and factories to back them up was not yet an intimate concern of national policy. Consequently that inadequate portion of our national technology devoted to military ends during peaceful years, would continue to produce a random trickle of military equipment. While such policies prevailed reasonable standards for U.S. defense could not be formulated in terms meaningful to military and technological planners.

CHAPTER IV

THE MILITARY DURING THE TWENTIES

WHEN THE A.E.F. CAME HOME FROM FRANCE, THE United States quickly reverted to its traditional handling of military affairs. In "winding up" the war, America's penchant for a "final solution" of difficult and continuing problems again asserted itself. The U.S. had just fought a conflict with the aim of ending all wars. Yet harsh postwar realities soon marred the utopia in whose name we had marched into battle. When the Wilsonian solution for assuring peace—the League of Nations—was compromised by our allies' demand for revenge and the spoils of victory, we turned our back to the perplexing problems of Europe and retreated once again into comfortable isolation.

Feast or Famine Pattern Recurs

A serious effort was made to capitalize on the experiences of the war, an effort reflected in the National Defense Act of 1920. But almost as soon as the lessons were forged into improved legislation they passed into limbo. The old pattern of feast or famine in military preparedness reasserted itself. Neglect of the Army was compounded of many things: the fear of standing armies, a preference for state militia over professional military forces, and continued reliance on the Navy as the first line of defense.

Domestic problems monopolized our attention. The tidal wave of anti-Bolshevik emotions which swept the country in the early twenties, prompted by such events as the bombing of J. P. Morgan Company and symbolized by the Mitchell Palmer investigations, proved to be a major distraction. Prohibition and gangsterism created new and exciting issues. Soon the burgeoning prosperity of the twenties beckoned the American people into a frenzied hunt for personal rewards.

The postwar revolt against everything military was reflected in the rebellion of the "lost generation." The problems of American security were buried under an avalanche of pacifist literature. President Calvin Coolidge allegedly squelched pleas for an increase in U.S. air power with the question, "Who's gonna fight us?" Apocryphal or fact, the attitude was typical of the time.

Nor did President Coolidge hesitate to air his antimilitarist views before men whose duty it was to safeguard the nation. In June 1925, he urged the graduating class of the Naval Academy at Annapolis to devote their first attention to the civilian life of the nation. "I am not unfamiliar," he said, "with the claim that if only we had a sufficient Military Establishment no one would ever molest us." But, he added: "I know of no nation in history that has ever been able to attain that position. I see no reason to expect that we could be the exception."[1]

[1] Address U. S. Naval Academy, June 3, 1925.

Education and Disarmament

The American people took on faith the naïve belief that another war was impossible—a belief which was not shaken by their government's refusal to join the League of Nations, the one organization dedicated, at least ostensibly, to the preservation of world peace. Military matters were pushed far into the background. American educators encouraged this tendency, and a generation of Americans grew up psychologically ill equipped to face the bitter conflict in which they were destined to participate.

"An increasing number of college professors and students," wrote Arthur A. Ekirch, Jr., "together with sympathetic allies in the churches and peace societies, began a far-reaching campaign against military training in schools and colleges. To co-ordinate this effort and to help arouse public interest, a group of liberal educators and pacifists formed the Committee on Militarism in Education. Educators and leaders of the peace movement had long agreed that, if war was to be abolished, American youth *would have to be trained to think in terms of peace and internationalism*. The presence of military training in schools and colleges was hardly compatible with this idea."[2]

A survey of undergraduate opinion during the early twenties indicated that the greater part of American college youth was opposed to large armaments and compulsory military service, including enforced drill in the colleges.[3]

[2] Arthur A. Ekirch, Jr., *The Civilian and the Military*, Oxford University Press, 1956, p. 220, italics supplied.

[3] Eliot Porter, "Student Opinion on War" (MS. Ph.D. dissertation, University of Chicago, 1926).

Perhaps more surprising was the enthusiasm for disarmament exhibited at this time by leading American military figures. In an address in New York before the European Relief Council, General John J. Pershing expressed alarm over expenditures for preparedness. "The lessons of the last six years should convince everybody of the danger of nations striding up and down the earth armed to the teeth. But no one nation can reduce armaments unless all do."[4]

Under these circumstances, it would have been a miracle if a viable U.S. military policy had evolved. The inescapable dependence of sound military policy upon equally sound and clearly defined national political objectives continued to be ignored, as it had been through most of our nation's history. The Army possessed a General Staff system, thanks largely to Elihu Root, which had rendered services, especially in France, out of all proportion to its size in World War I. That staff system had been strengthened by legislation in 1920. Yet military planning was impossible in the absence of guiding directives, in other words, a national policy, from the civilian chiefs. The Navy, unprepared for major extended operations far from U.S. shores, still lacked both a unified command and a co-ordinated logistic organization. Nearly twenty years would pass before the warnings of the Hepburn Board, appointed in 1938 to review the status of the U. S. Fleet, stimulated long overdue changes in the eleventh hour before World War II.

As is often the case, the losing side learned the most from the First World War. Its salient lesson could be summed up in a single proposition: weapons, all other things being equal, provide the key to victory. "Strategy, command, leadership, courage, discipline, supply, organization, and all

[4] New York *Times* (Dec. 30, 1920).

the moral and physical paraphernalia of war are nothing to high superiority weapons—at most they go to form the one per cent which makes the whole possible . . .

"In war, especially in modern wars, in which weapons change rapidly, one thing is certain; no army of 50 years before any date selected would stand a dog's chance against the army existing at that date . . . Generally speaking it is machine power, not manpower which wins. A side that improves its weapons more rapidly is the side which eventually is going to win. Nevertheless, so untechnically minded were any of the Western powers between the two World Wars, that little attempt was made to mold their Armed Forces around the fact that weapons are the decisive factor."[5]

The Public and Congress

The U.S. focussed its postwar critique on the organization of the armed forces. It was blind to the fact that the last war had been as much a struggle between factories and laboratories as between massed armies. The main fruit of Congressional pondering was the National Defense Act of 1920. This amendment of the 1916 Act established the U. S. Military System on a solid foundation in the tradition of small standing forces and maximum utilization of citizen-reserves. Yet nothing on the record indicates that American Presidents or Congressmen ever attempted to put flesh on this sound structure.

By 1922 Congress had so cut appropriations that the Act was vitiated. Almost twenty years elapsed before the Army attained the size authorized by the Act. During the decade

[5] J. F. C. Fuller, *Armament and History*, Scribner's, 1954, p. 18.

of the twenties, no Congressman lost his seat because of his lack of interest in the armed forces. Nor was the security of the U.S. seriously mentioned in the platform of either party. Still, all things considered, the National Defense Act did represent a new and on the whole progressive military charter for the U. S. Army. Most people at the time agreed with the appraisal of General Peyton C. March, World War I Chief of Staff, that this Act capitalized on the experience of the war and represented sound military policy. This legislation recognized that warfare was now waged from an industrial base, that "God was on the side with the big factories." Technology as the creator and purveyor of industrial power seems to have been taken for granted.

The belated recognition of industry's role in warfare was embodied in the newly created office of Assistant Secretary of War, charged with supervising procurement of all military supplies and preparations for wartime industrial mobilization. This first break in the U.S. tradition of stripping our war-built military machine of its vital parts at the termination of each conflict initially received little serious attention. Its immediate result was War Department confusion over division of the General Staff's and Assistant Secretary's responsibilities, resolved in 1921 by the Harbord Board, of which more below. A subsequent step was the founding of the Army Industrial College in 1924.

Congress almost immediately proceeded to undercut the Act's effectiveness by purse-tightening. In 1921, funds limited the strength of the Army to 120,000, although 280,000 had been authorized the previous year. By 1927 the budget set Army strength at 118,000 men, not much greater than the force of 100,000 allowed a disarmed Germany by the Treaty of Versailles.

America Foreswears Command of the Sea

Nor did the Navy fare much better under the dual impact of economy and the celebrated Disarmament Conference of 1922. This conference had a curious origin in the convictions of President Wilson. At the end of World War I, only the United States was in a position to challenge Britain's naval preponderance. America's challenge was inspired by Wilson's passionate conviction that his Fourteen Points were the key to genuine peace. The second of these points spelled out "absolute freedom of navigation upon the seas, outside territorial waters, alike in peace and war." This point denied the legality of blockade itself, to say nothing of the venerable custom of search on the high seas and seizure of contraband. The British had no interest in Wilson's principle. In fact, they opposed it. The allies ignored it at the peace conference.

Wilson, smarting under this rebuff, decided upon unilateral action. When the Navy's building program was up for consideration in 1919 by the General Board, Wilson gave his personal blessing to a request to Congress that would double the heavy 1916 schedule. The new building program would have meant a fleet of over 50 first-line vessels, utterly overshadowing the British Navy.

It is not known whether or not Wilson really expected to obtain the necessary appropriations, but foreign fears that the U.S. would carry out the program ultimately led to the holding of the disarmament conference. The results were a setback for the U. S. Navy. New construction was halted and its best ships scrapped to attain "parity" with the British, who sank only obsolete battleships. The partially completed battlecruisers which were towed out to sea from Newport News and scuttled had been rated by Jane's international naval encyclopedia as the world's most powerful fighting ships.

Another result of the conference was the U.S. decision to forego the development of Pacific naval bases in Guam and the Philippines. This decision in effect insured Japanese naval supremacy in the Far East. Whether or not the American delegation was bargaining away empty rights is a moot question; Congress would probably never have implemented a decision to construct strong bases in either Guam or the Philippines. Both these possessions had been in American hands for twenty-three years with nothing significant having been done toward their protection in the event of war.

Leaders Ignore Technology

The reduction of our naval forces was not the only symptom of America's penchant for regarding international treaties as a valid substitute for national defense. We continued to extoll world-wide peace as the objective of our foreign policy, while, at the same time, neglecting the military power which might have lent strength to our exhortations. Thus we straggled once again into the quandary of attempting to fashion foreign policy from morality alone.

Civilian and military leaders blithely ignored the changes technology was working in global strategy. Franklin D. Roosevelt assured the readers of *Asia* magazine in 1923 that a war between the U.S. and Japan was almost unthinkable because geography rendered it out of the question. Based on his experiences as Assistant Secretary of the Navy, he concluded that any attempt at hostilities would result in "Japan and the U.S. . . . making faces at one another across no man's water as broad as the Pacific." Such fixed opinions tended to insulate national policy against the impact of new technology and new weapons.

The armed forces had fallen on lean days. They experienced a continual drop in manpower. For weapons they depended almost entirely on stocks of unused equipment left over from the First World War and rapidly becoming obsolete because of the fast pace of a booming industrial technology.

Congress persistently barred the Treasury against the military's attempts to benefit by new technologies. During the twenties the War Department repeatedly sought to place small "educational orders" for a few items that would have to be produced in large quantities in the event of war. These proposals to spend only two million dollars a year were direct, if unduly modest, responses to the responsibility recently imposed by Congress upon the newly created Assistant Secretary of War for Industrial Mobilization. All such plans were defeated.

In retrospect the reasons are not difficult to discover. The appropriations sought were too small to attract the interested support of any industry. Not yet accustomed to doing business with the government, industry, under the conditions of prosperity then existing, would not have pressured Congress for even unjustifiably large orders. Government contracts are avidly sought only during a depression or when government purchases constitute the product's principal outlet. Conversely, the greater gains from private sales always attract manufacturers while "business is good" as it was during the "roaring twenties."

Prosperity Bypasses the Military

The country's small military establishment was caught in a tightening vise of military austerity and domestic prosperity. Pay scales, unchanged since 1908 save for a temporary wartime raise revoked in 1922, had fallen far below those of industry. Desertion rates were high among the drifters and ne'er-do-wells who comprised a large percentage of applicants at recruiting stations. Many brilliant officers, notably aviators Eugene Wilson, Jimmy Doolittle, and engineers C. E. Lohr and Sherwood Cheney, foresook their careers for lucrative positions in civilian life.

Army units, including those of the National Guard, could not engage in joint maneuvers, even on the modest scale before World War I, because of lack of funds. Ammunition for target practice came from deteriorating wartime leftovers, parsimoniously doled out. While trucks replaced horse-drawn wagons throughout the nation, the tired mule remained the Army's chief means of transportation. The 1918 Liberty truck, produced too late for service in France, cost more than its value in maintenance. Precious money was spent on converting some Liberty trucks from solid to pneumatic tires—money which should have been used to purchase more useful vehicles.

The dollar shortage was not the sole reason for the erosion of our military power during the twenties. True, the failure of Congress to appropriate sufficient money had a stagnating effect. Yet, the military was handcuffed in its efforts to use intelligently even those modest funds at its disposal. The dispersal of the Army throughout the country not only hampered training, as already observed, but also imposed a formidable housekeeping burden. Yet repeated War Department efforts to cut down the inordinate number of small, uneconomic Army posts were invariably defeated by Congressmen who jealously insisted upon retaining every installation in their own constituencies.

Throughout this period the Navy received priority treatment, such as it was, in defense funds. The famous aircraft carriers *Lexington* and *Saratoga* were commissioned late in 1927 following a 1926 authorization to increase the Navy's operational aircraft to 1000 over a five-year period. The *Ranger*, first U.S. ship designed from keel up as a carrier, was authorized in 1929, though not commissioned until 1934. No other fleet-type ships were built despite repeated complaints by the Navy Department regarding the deficiency in cruisers below treaty strength.

Even so, the Navy's persistent claim to be the first line of defense made it increasingly difficult for the Army's case to be heard. Neither the War or Navy Departments received White House support for their programs. In a political atmosphere of peace and economy, defense appropriations were the easiest to pare down. Presidential recommendations to Congress on military budgets were invariably lower than those proposed by the services.

The paucity of public interest in military affairs, technological or otherwise, was typified by a so-called "test of industrial preparedness" in the fall of 1924 under the chairmanship of Judge Elbert H. Gary, head of the U. S. Steel Corporation. The test concentrated upon the time it would take to produce ordnance items and airplanes which "being noncommercial production were most difficult to procure." There is no evidence that the weaknesses of our mobilization schemes revealed by the "test" resulted in any action by either the government, industry, or the War Department.

In this wilderness several voices were heard but unheeded. Dr. Herman Schneider, Engineering Dean at the University of Cincinnati, published in 1924 in the Army Ordnance magazine his findings regarding World War I transportation. Dr. Schneider decided that the factory shutdowns, ordered by the U. S. Coal Commissioner in January 1918, initially for one week and at the rate of one day a week for some weeks thereafter, were caused by "ignorance of railroad congestion certain to result from procedures in placing war orders." The one-way flow of materials from west to east made transportation the limiting factor in national resources. This condition, Dr. Schneider warned, still prevailed. Nevertheless, the war-born Army Transportation Corps created to handle such problems and disbanded in 1920, was not reinstated until the greater emergency of World War II arose.

Technological Environment

The surge of technology preceding World War I picked up momentum during the conflict and, spreading into many new lines, spurred development of devices still in their comparative infancy. Because of this acceleration the telephone, automobile, the motion picture, the radio, and the airplane became commonplace throughout the United States during the twenties. By these instrumentalities, technology changed our way of life.

It is hard to visualize now, for example, that in 1920 comparatively few cities had all their streets paved; that paved roads between cities were rare and, in the countryside, scarcely existed. Today, the highways that crisscross our continent are the very sinews of our way of life. So too, sectional barriers within the nation have crumbled under the impact of the revolution in communications media.

After a nation's economy reaches the threshold of industrial maturity, the rate of technological advance accelerates. This hastened pace was evident in the U.S. during the decade of Harding and Coolidge. Yet the great strides made in the fields mentioned had almost no contemporary impact on our military services. For example, radio developed commercially between the two World Wars to a higher degree in America than in any other country—but not in the communications networks of our armed forces. The possibility of radar was known in this country for a number of years in advance of World War II. Yet, since there appeared to be no profitable application of this discovery, practically nothing was done to develop it.

Similarly, the progress in automotive transportation was not paralleled by improvements in military transport. Little or no money was made available to the services for their own development in these fields. At the same time private business, impelled by the all-eclipsing profit motive, put its research funds to work only in support of ideas which promised a sure return.

In 1926 a compilation of eleven years' work by Dr. Robert H. Goddard of Clark University in Worcester, Massachusetts, experimenting with rockets became available. He had successfully fired the first rocket powered by a liquid fuel motor, five years ahead of the earliest German competitor. For more than a decade Goddard's "unprofitable" research received attention only in Hitler's Reich. Also about this time a joint Army-Navy project in flying pilotless aircraft was abandoned as "unpromising," for lack of funds.

These examples typify the lassitude of the interwar period —the time that was wasted and the opportunities that were missed. As a nation we failed to realize the responsibility of the government for tapping the scientific and industrial resources of our economy in the interest of over-all security.

Technology Remakes Civilian America

It is illuminating to scan the areas in which technology was remaking American life during the twenties with little or no influence on matters military. The following list of accomplishments is extracted from *America's Needs and Resources:*[6] "Construction materials, electric equipment, food preparation, clothing and fabrics, synthetics, chemical methods, motor trucks, airplanes, health and medical care, medical equipment, radio and television, motion pictures, mechanization of agriculture, soil structure, pest control, electrification, internal combustion engines, transportation techniques, equipment handling, materials handling, conveyor belts, paper and printing machines."

Startling progress was made in all these fields of technology in the U.S. of the twenties. Yet until the outbreak of World War II, the impact of this progress upon the military, particularly the Army, was negligible. For example, radios designed by the Signal Corps laboratories in the late thirties were technically behind commercial models. The inventory of obsolescent equipment, to which the Army was fettered

[6] J. Frederic Dewhurst and associates, *America's Needs and Resources; A New Survey*, The Twentieth Century Fund, New York, 1955, Chapter 24.

by financial restrictions, isolated the Army, technologically speaking, from contemporary American economy.

There was no program to harness science to military development. The Army and Navy had almost no research and development funds. American industry, uninterested in military contracts, was making ever greater use of scientific research in its own operations. Within a score of years after the World War, research was animating every major industrial process in the country. A systematic attack upon the technological problems replaced the hit-and-miss approach by the lonely inventors of former times.

This research by "teamwork" became commonplace among the bigger U.S. companies following World War I. Highly organized laboratories owned by such massive concerns as General Electric[7] and Du Pont, generously endowed with resources and equipment, blueprinted the technological achievements which transformed this country into an industrial giant.

A similar effort devoted to the solution of the military's technological problems would have radically changed the character of the two World Wars. Almost every idea which later proved significant when tested on the battlefield was available before the wars began. Prior to 1914, for example, the gasoline engine, machine gun, the airplane and radio were all available. Between wars the Germans organized their forces around the tank, the airplane, and radio communications and with this combination scored their smashing victories in the early stages of World War II. No such unified weapons concept existed in our Army.

[7] General Electric was in the forefront of the trend toward organized Research & Development. By 1957 this one company was putting $250,000,-000 a year into R&D.

What was lacking was comprehension in peacetime America that war would change as technology changed. Although the "partnership between the soldier, the miner, the technician and the scientist is an ancient one,"[8] this European truism had never applied to the pattern of American growth.

The Military Overlooks a "Mule"

Nor was the military itself blameless. For example, an Ordnance Corps officer produced in 1920 a recognizable prototype of the famous cross-country vehicle, the "mule," which was to be hailed as "new" in 1956. This vehicle, designed to transport infantrymen and their weapons over all kinds of terrain, is regarded as a major advance by footslogging soldiers. Yet its forgotten ancestor of a quarter of a century ago was actually superior. It floated! In short, military myopia, inability to look beyond the economy-strapped present, prevented technological advances, occurring so rapidly in the civilian community, from being applied to military requirements.

By 1930, government and private industry were spending $140,000,000 a year for scientific research. In the same period, the Army's budget for research and development averaged some $4,600,000. Had the U.S. funneled money into the development of radar, rockets and comparable devices between the wars, there is little doubt that the history of World War II would have been different. Avenues that might profitably have been explored include: location of hostile artil-

[8] *Technics and Civilization*, Lewis Mumford, Harcourt Brace, 1934, p. 87.

lery by sound ranging, improved radio communications, cross-country vehicles, landing craft, flame throwers, prefabricated bridge material, harder armor, shaped-charge projectiles, land and marine mine developments, photographic equipment, diesel engines, improved traction, improved powders. Unfortunately, the tendency to keep an obsolete weapons inventory usable completely absorbed what paltry sums were available.

Our experience in World War I taught us that European science and industry had been giving constant attention to devising new weapons. From attachés and business contacts we learned that such development continued in Europe after the war and was well under way in Japan. Nevertheless, for whatever reasons, we averted our eyes from our foreign competitors and made little effort to keep abreast of them.

The Naval Story

Although the Navy continued to be the favored child in the American military family, its postwar decline paralleled in many respects that of its sister service. Postwar allegations that the Navy had possessed no realistic, operational plan to fight Germany and, by inference, similar shortcomings for the future, roused a brief storm because of their source, Admiral Sims, U. S. Commander of American naval operations in European waters, April 1917–March 1919. An inconclusive Congressional investigation put an end to the controversy outside the Navy itself though acrimonious professional argument subsided more slowly. Soon afterward, the shipbuilding holiday sponsored by the Washington treaties retarded ship design. The U.S. disarmament policy and an economy-minded Congress so stifled new construction, even to replace obsolescence, that the Navy dropped below authorized treaty strength. As with the Army, the repair and maintenance of the fleet had a priority claim on the limited funds available. But fortunately for the Navy, breaks occasionally came its way.

The 1928 elections over, President Coolidge astounded an Armistice Day audience with an address calling upon Congress to pass a fifteen-cruiser bill already rejected by the Senate. When the Senate assembled in December, both the cruiser bill and the Kellogg-Briand Pact for outlawing war were on the agenda at the same time. In February 1929, the cruiser bill was approved with the provision that the program might be suspended if the United States Government was able to negotiate a successful agreement for naval limitations. This the President was "requested to encourage."[9]

Thus buttressed by legislation, the Navy recorded some notable achievements in the decade before the war. Conversion of two battle cruiser hulls into the aircraft carriers *Lexington* and *Saratoga*, commissioned in 1927, made it possible to pioneer the operational technique of a fleet air arm. The world's first example of "strategic air power" was demonstrated in the winter of 1928–29 in naval maneuvers off Panama. The carrier *Saratoga* with a miniature "task force" simulated a predawn "sneak attack" on the Canal locks in the face of vastly superior "conventional" naval forces. Unnoticed beyond a small professional circle, this operation authorized by Admiral Joseph M. Reeves was described by Admiral William B. Pratt, Commander in Chief of the U. S. Fleet, as "the most brilliantly conceived and effectively

[9] Congressional Record, 70th Congress, 2nd Session, 678–9, 2599, 2619.

executed naval operation in our history," and, prophetically, "destined to revolutionize naval warfare."[10]

In quite a different medium asdic, the underwater detection device which developed into sonar, made possible the detection of submarines from surface ships. This development was painstakingly and ably fostered, perhaps because it involved relatively low costs and promised a new weapon of readily recognized high tactical utility.

The U. S. Fleet completed conversion to oil fuel shortly after the First World War. This conversion was exploited by new techniques for refueling underway at sea with consequent extension of the fleet's operating range. Simultaneously, fire-control systems were radically improved and the vulnerability of powder magazines to a direct hit on a gun turret—which caused the loss of British battle cruisers at Jutland—was eliminated. On the whole the American Navy compared favorably with that of the other naval powers in terms of advancing technology.

The Navy lacked enough cruisers because of insufficient naval bases as well as inadequate appropriations. This former deficiency resulted from a policy penchant to view our sea arm as a purely defensive force. We forgot that British bases had made the U. S. Fleet effective in 1917–18 and we continued to neglect Mahan's comprehensive guide lines to sea power.

The Army's Record

Operating under the 1920 Act, the reorganized Army stumbled into the postwar decade with a major blunder. Its

[10] *Wings of the Dawn*, E. E. Wilson, Stone Book Connecticut Printer.

1921 Mobilization Plan proposed a force of six and a half million men to be drafted, equipped and trained in the nineteen months following M day. Munitions to support this plan would have cost, according to the estimate of the Assistant Chief of Staff (G-4), $5 billion and could not be produced by U.S. industry in the stipulated time. The newly created office of Assistant Secretary of War was to be charged with the responsibility of industrial mobilization for remedying this last defect. The immensity of the proposed program invited caustic rebuff from an economy-minded Congress and administration. Although "information on the foreign policy of the U.S. does not appear to have been available to the War Department,"[11] this scarcely excuses the Staff planners for sponsoring a program so far beyond conceivable defense needs at the time. The grandiose plan was brusquely shelved. Had it been made public it would have amplified the clamor against "militarism" that defeated the proposal for a 500,000-man regular Army in 1919.

This experience seemed to have a profound impact upon General Staff planners. Later mobilization plans became sufficiently "realistic" politically to allow Staff officers to do at least some paper work, though these plans too remained essentially dead letters. Twenty years later that Staff's successors had become so conditioned to timid "realism" that they were utterly unable, even when given a free hand, to foresee the need for an army one-third the size brashly proposed in 1921.

However, the Army made some brave attempts toward progress in the recently recognized industrialization of war-

[11] *History of Military Mobilization in the U. S. Army,* Kreidberg and Henry, Government Printing Office, 1955, p. 389.

fare. The Harbord Board, headed by Major General James G. Harbord, promptly resolved the apparent conflict of responsibilities between the new Assistant Secretary and the General Staff. The General Staff, in its planning function, was to furnish Army requirements to the former. The Assistant Secretary's office would employ these requirements as a basis for his industrial mobilization program, in which he would supervise the Army's Technical Services' work in procurement and detailed supply planning.

Unfortunately until 1939, no specific budget allocation was ever given the Assistant Secretary to prosecute his duties. In the twenties he was estimated to have spent annually between $100,000 and $350,000 (general funds) for procurement planning. As in the past, Congress declined to appropriate money for "educational orders" to industry.

An Army "Business" Education

Stymied in concrete achievements, the Army made substantial strides in theory, at least. In 1924, Secretary of War John W. Weeks established the Army Industrial College[12] to conduct research and instruct officers in the business, if not exactly the technological, aspects of warfare. Quickly expanded to a full year course and receiving a few naval officers in each class, the college regularly heard lectures from business leaders who, the records show, spoke freely in the closed

[12] The Secretary's speech at the opening was titled "We Need a New Mahan to Write the Influence of Industry upon History." He claimed it was "captious to criticize military authority for not exercising greater prevision than industrial leaders" citing the "slow emergence and development by experience" of great inventions such as the steam engine and the automobile.

sessions on the knotty problems involved in military-industrial relations. In the decade of the thirties, treated in the following chapter, the Industrial College produced blueprints for industrial mobilization which were repeatedly revised and improved.

Another essential purpose was furthered by the college: co-operative planning by the Army and Navy, especially aimed at eliminating the time and money wasted by competitive procurement between the two services. The Army and Navy Munitions Board was created in 1922 for that specific purpose by a joint action of the Secretaries of War and Navy. Just as the logistic responsibilities of the Industrial College paralleled the strategic studies of the War College, this Board was intended to complement the operational planning of Army and Navy Joint Board. Lacking any real authority and functioning under the long shadows which Presidential disfavor cast upon the Joint Board, the Munitions Board scored little success during the twenties. Under its charter, this agency considered only military requirements. No civilian counterpart existed to estimate civilian consumption without which a thorough study of industrial mobilization was impossible.

With regard to awareness of technological developments' impact upon military affairs, the Army seems in retrospect to have been more sinned against than sinning. The Army school system was now fully developed with service schools for each combat arm and technical service, the Command and General Staff School (renamed in 1923 and 1928 without change in status), the Army War College and the already cited Industrial College. That the technological aspects of instruction, normally predominantly logistical, lacked the prestige of tactical courses might be inferred from the fact that the top man in each class at the Industrial College was awarded a place in the next year's class at the War College, though on paper their curricula were "equal" in importance. However, students in all the schools received instruction in the more modern equipment, usually prototypes of modern items such as tanks, armored cars, bridging equipage and improved field guns scarce or nonexistent among the troop units to which they returned. At Fort Benning, Fort Sill, and other training centers "school troops," especially selected companies or battalions, worked with and demonstrated the newest equipment. Unfortunately, upon departure from the military "campus," graduates could follow the operational employment of these modest developments only by reading.

Improvement in Weapons Selection

The Army's internal organization for making decisions regarding weapons selection improved during the twenties. Far into the First World War the Chief of Ordnance had retained almost complete authority for such decisions. The implications of this control can be seen in the ups and downs of American tank development. The first armored automobile built in the United States was developed in 1915 by Col. R. P. Davidson. Before America's entry into the First World War, tanks had attracted official attention, and the American Military Mission in Paris was directed to investigate the subject. The report prepared by this commission stressed the effects of the machines in use but paid little attention to the principle of armored mobility. In other words, the initial American attitude was surprisingly skeptical. However, a board appointed by General Pershing in July 1917 recommended among other things that "tanks should be considered an important factor in war . . . there should be centralized control over tank matters."

Subsequently, under Ordnance supervision many thousand tanks were ordered in the United States prior to the Armistice. When a test was made in France to determine the character of their armor, it could not stop heavy-caliber bullets. There was a solid lack of communication of technical information between Europe and the U.S. Much of the mechanical experience gained by the Allies was ignored, practically all the models built were of mediocre design and doomed to failure.

As a result of this kind of experience, the Army's troop leaders began to play a much greater role in determining the military characteristics of new weapons as well as in judging whether a particular weapon met stipulated requirements. For example, the 1925 report of the Chief of Ordnance stated that manufacture of the new 105-mm howitzer carriage had not been settled "between box-trail or split-trail carriage types" and then indicated that "Tests [to determine the choice] have been ordered by the Field Artillery."

Much has been made of the fact that the Ordnance Department neglected to follow, much less pace, progress in foreign countries. This failure, like equivalent ones in World War I, became public knowledge only as the Second World War was being fought by other nations.

One might ask whether any military establishment could have accomplished greater things under the severe fiscal handicaps imposed. Army Ordnance appropriations for 1924 were approximately *one-half what had been made available in 1910.* This sum constituted less than 3 per cent of the entire War Department appropriation. Since the Ordnance

Department represents the combat equipment side of the Army, the devastating restrictions imposed by budgetary limitations can be readily seen. As the *History of Army Ordnance in World War II* indicates (pages 31–32), "from 1920–1940 plans had always to be shaved down, operations were always restricted, projects were frequently stopped short of completion, all for lack of money." More money was going into the preservation of outmoded World War I equipment than in the development or purchase of new.

The truism that the most effective weapons of any conflict result from time-consuming prewar developments was cherished, almost unavailingly, by a few consecrated officers. As fruits of their toil, for example, Fort Tilden, New York, possessed by 1924 two 16-inch barbette-mount guns which fired a 2340-pound projectile capable of penetrating 14-inch armor at an extreme range of 31 miles. These weapons, manufactured at the Watervliet Arsenal, were without peer in the military world, yet ten years passed before funds permitted others like them to be installed in the defenses of Panama and Pearl Harbor. By that time their value in the face of aerial bombing was beginning to be doubtful.[13]

In 1925 a thousand members of the American Chemical Society viewing a demonstration at the Aberdeen Proving Ground were "impressed by the remarkable strides since World War I."[14] They saw "ultramodern" tanks, the new 16-inch gun (*supra*), a 14-inch railroad gun, a new dirigible (the TC-21), parachute jumps, experimental cross-country

---

[13] As an ironic technological footnote, a battery of these monster weapons was being dug into the seaside cliffs north of the Golden Gate in 1939. The plan was to emplace the guns in tunnel openings, invulnerable to air attack. Before work was completed, the futility of fixed emplacements to defend a large port finally became recognized. The project was dropped.

[14] *Ordnance* magazine, March–April 1925.

vehicles. At the same time, the report of the Chief of Ordnance noted that redesign of matériel had been limited in
1924 to "one type of tank, and the smallest caliber of antiaircraft guns." For 1925, he continued, even this must be
dropped. An *Ordnance* magazine editorial mildly deprecated
this parsimony. No protest emanated from the tycoons
listed as trustees for the Ordnance Association, which included many of America's most prominent captains of industry.

The Controversy over Air Power

The only military equipment maturing during World War
I that drew and held the attention of the U. S. Government
and the American public at large was the airplane. Under the
stress of Fokker bombing raids on London, Britain had
created the Royal Air Force in 1917, the first independent
Air Arm in military annals. Over the battle zone, American
experiments in massing aircraft borrowed from our Allies
had suggested startling tactical potentials for supporting
ground troops. Late in the conflict, U.S. fliers had heartily
endorsed the R.A.F.'s plans for bombardment aircraft to attack the Ruhr if the war continued into 1919. In naval aviation Britain, with the first operational aircraft carriers, led all
others.

Organizationally, military aviation had grown far beyond
its prewar fledgling status. The U. S. Army Air Service,
created by General Pershing in the A.E.F., replaced the incongruous Aviation Section of the Signal Corps with its obsolete fixation upon only one mission of air power: observation. By 1921, Congress authorized the Navy to establish a

Bureau of Aeronautics, superseding the section, in the Chief of Naval Operations office, previously charged with naval aviation.

Already a naval aircraft, the NC-4, had made history in May 1919, by flying the Atlantic, via Newfoundland and the Azores; a seaplane tender (USS *Wright*) had been commissioned; and the first U.S. carrier (USS *Langley*), a converted collier, was placed in service in March 1922. Complementary progress featured Admiral Bradley A. Fiske's pioneer work with the aerial torpedo which resulted in successful torpedo-bomber planes being built at the Naval Aircraft Factory in 1923 and a year later by Douglas.

Bombers Versus Battleships

Meanwhile, Brigadier General William Mitchell plunged the Army Air Service into a controversy over the effectiveness of aerial bombing as justification for his demands for an independent Air Force. Congressional hearings led to two tests of air versus naval power in 1921 and 1923. In the earlier series, new Martin bombers carrying the first 2000-pound bombs (developed in four months by Army Ordnance) bombed the German battleship *Ostfriedland* along with older and smaller vessels. In the later tests, naval aircraft bombed two old U.S. battleships and the incomplete battle-cruiser *Washington*, which had been marked for destruction by the 1922 Naval Disarmament Treaty. The results were interpreted by U.S. authorities to substantiate the invulnerability of capital ships against air attack even when delivered by improved aircraft. This conclusion was dramatically reversed early in 1942 when Japanese bombers sank two of

Britain's stanchest battleships in waters off the Malaya Peninsula.

Concurrent development in lighter-than-air craft centered around two huge rigid airships, both built for the Navy by Germany's Zeppelin Company as part of war reparations. Increased production of helium, a wartime U.S. "first," eliminated the risks of using explosive hydrogen for buoyancy. Nevertheless, when one of these ships, the *Shenandoah*, crashed in a violent storm along the Ohio River in September 1925, enthusiasm for airships dropped close to zero.

In the same month two Navy patrol airplanes attempted to fly from California to Hawaii. One was quickly forced down and rescued, but the crew of the other disappeared at sea where, resourcefully sailing their seaplane, they were picked up ten days later within ten miles of their destination.

During the clamor attending these mishaps, General Mitchell publicly charged "incompetency, criminal negligence, and almost treasonable administration of our national defense by the Navy and War Departments."[15] This outburst brought the famous court-martial and conviction of Mitchell, who resigned from the Army. More important, it virtually compelled the administration to take action. President Coolidge appointed a Board of Inquiry, headed by Dwight W. Morrow, to investigate the status of military and civilian aviation in the U.S.

The Board, in proceedings which lasted three months, heard countless witnesses. It rejected proposals for a consolidated aviation organization but recommended Assistant Secretaries for Aeronautics in the War, Navy, and Commerce Departments. Government manufacture of air-

[15] *Navy Wings*, U. S. Navy Dept., NAVPERS 10822-A, Government Printing Office, 1955, p. 23.

craft, other than experimental work, was disapproved. Stand-ardization of designs for three years were sought so industry might build up a reserve of planes. Helpful to the struggling aircraft industry in need of volume production this procedure would handicap technological improvement of American aviation.

The Board's recommendations guided U.S. policy on air power for years. As a prompt first step, Congress authorized the three subcabinet posts, created the Army Air Corps (in-stead of "Service") equal to Infantry and Artillery arms, and ordered a five-year building program for both Army and Navy aviation. Nevertheless, Commander Richard E. Byrd was compelled to obtain private financial backing for his trail-blazing flight over the North Pole in the same year, although Congress saw fit to recognize the feat by bestowing medals and promotion upon Byrd and his pilot.

Out of Bitterness, Aeronautics

The controversy over air power in the twenties, for all its bitterness, aided the technological development of the U.S. military establishment. The men who fought for air power were imaginative enthusiasts. Senior Army and Navy officers in general saw aircraft as a limited, auxiliary weapon. The enthusiasts argued in terms of aircraft and equipment which they did not possess and had little real chance of getting for years to come. While many of the so-called principles of future war—for example, the one that bombardment of its cities would force a nation to capitulate—laid down by Mitchell and his followers proved false in the circumstances of the Second World War, these men were far ahead of their critics in foreseeing the possibilities which technology did bring to the range and scope of airpower.

Though outwardly subdued, air-power separatists in both services continued their long struggle with different results. When the smoke of World War II cleared away, a Washington wag explained: "The Army aviators fought twenty-seven years to become independent of the War Department, while the Navy fliers simply took over the whole Navy at least a dozen years sooner."

The Morrow Board rightly concluded: "There is no present reason for apprehension of any invasion by air." Their forecast was less prophetic: "Nor indeed is there any apparent probability of such an invasion in the future which can be foreseen." The central point, that changing technology affects war and strategy, often disastrously to the unheeding, was lost in the welter of charges, countercharges and bureaucratic stand-patism.

Although technology was one of the primary forces influencing the development of American society during the decade following the First World War, this technology had little or no influence on the structure and character of the American armed forces, which, in turn, had almost no impact on the conduct of our foreign affairs. The nation and science forgot war and forgot the military. The military, with exceptions, were complacent. A few dedicated men, bright and easy to see against a dull background, carried on and some institutional reforms were made. The government and the people of the U.S. were far from realizing that periods of low military budgets should be periods of great emphasis upon weapons quality.

CHAPTER V

TECHNOLOGY AND MILITARY POLICY
DURING THE THIRTIES

JANUARY 1930 FOUND THE UNITED STATES IN A STATE OF shock induced by the stock market crash of October 1929. Despite some enlightened fiscal legislation and the solid progress of industrial technology, that were presumably to have eliminated financial panics, the United States sank rapidly into a deep depression. Hard times persisted, ironically, until the world-wide tragedy of war restored "prosperity."

The decade's first two years were the last two of the Hoover administration, whose spokesmen hopefully suggested that "prosperity was right around the corner." That administration continued its slogan of "normalcy" in the nation's affairs while relying unsuccessfully upon a policy of letting natural forces bring about a business recovery. The trend toward governmental economy which had been a basic aim of both the Coolidge and Hoover administrations was emphasized by the stringency of the depression and stultified even the military's low-gear effort to match spectacular progress of science in industry.

148

The early thirties also marked the high point of popular revulsion toward the First World War as characterized by such a book and film as *All Quiet on the Western Front* and R. C. Sherriff's powerful play *Journey's End*. Condemnation of war was matched by emotional demands to "take the profits out of war" in the event this country was ever again forced into conflict. Considerable popular pressure, originating from such diverse sources as the American Legion and the *Christian Science Monitor*, led President Hoover to create a "War Policy Commission" whose task was to "study and consider amending the Constitution" to permit government seizure of private property in wartime (but not the conscription of labor). This commission consisted of eight Congressional and six Cabinet appointees. Just before the end of President Hoover's incumbency in 1932, the War Policies Commission reported on two positive programs which might conceivably achieve its assigned objectives. These were the War Department's Industrial Mobilization Plan of 1930 which was the first full-scale mobilization plan prepared by the Army Industrial College and the Baruch Plan which was an alternative suggested by a distinguished citizen with first-hand experience in the mechanics and problems of wartime mobilizations.

The War Department Industrial Mobilization Plan of 1930, sponsored by Assistant Secretary of War Frederick H. Payne and Army Chief of Staff General Douglas MacArthur, was essentially a procurement plan, in outline only, that was subsequently fleshed out and extended in repeated editions. In its outline form, it covered such matters as priorities, price control, commandeering industrial plants, foreign trade, and U.S. government corporations. It suggested wartime appointment of "czars" for industry, labor, selective service, and public relations. It stated that "control of industry in war is a Presidential function, exercised through civilian agencies" and that its success "depended upon public opinion."

The two basic proposals commented upon by the commission differed mainly in procedures recommended. Baruch insisted that a ceiling be imposed upon *all* prices and that civilian officials handle advanced planning, a function previously carried out by the military. The Army Industrial College's proposal, in its turn, reflected confidence in military incorruptability and suspicion of business and labor lobbies. Critical evaluations of the real merits of both proposals were ignored in the partisan discussion that ensued in Congress. A minority report of Representative Ross A. Collins of Mississippi charged that the Industrial College Plan for mobilization implied "regulation of civilian life by the Army and Navy." Action upon the commission's findings, whichever plan was followed, would have brought modern industry into some degree of partnership with the Armed Services and thus lifted the heavy hand of technological obsolescence which so long had stifled the nation's military establishment. Actually, nothing was done.

To a certain extent the War Policy Commission itself went beyond its task and recommended that a new mobilization plan, however prepared, be produced every two years and presented to Congress. This the Industrial College carried out during the decade. The commission also proposed a reorganization of the executive department of the government which was an intellectual forebearer of the so-called Hoover Reports to the President in the 1950s.

The timing could not have been more unfortunate. Apathy, economy, and unemployment combined to block

military progress and thought. According to General Mac-
Arthur, the United States Army then stood seventeenth in
rank, according to size, among the nations of the world. Naval appropriations had sunk to one-third of what they had
been in 1921. Consequently, though both plans dealing with
the mobilization of American industrial and technological
resources were in substantial agreement, little real consideration was given to their importance. Eventually they were
found to contain the basis for the mobilization procedures
followed by the government during World War II. Under
the pressure of the economic disaster neither the American
people nor their Congress paid much attention to the problems of military security that were to loom so large before
the decade was over.

Roosevelt Takes Command

By an odd coincidence in history, two men who were to be
the major protagonists in the Second World War assumed
the political leadership of the United States and Germany at
almost the same time, Franklin D. Roosevelt and Adolf
Hitler. Roosevelt was elected to the Presidency in protest to
the "laissez-faire" policies pursued by the Hoover administration in dealing with the depression. He also came to
office on a plank of government economy and retrench-
ment. He quickly found out that he could not reduce the
moneys made available to various vote-controlling cliques.
Consequently, the military forces were not only fair game
but politically the easiest targets for budget cuts. Political
opportunism, however, soon ran into a snag. Both the Army
and Navy budgets had already been trimmed to the bone by

the "Coolidge Economy" which President Hoover had continued. War Department appropriations of those years included civil works funds, chiefly the rivers and harbors, so-called "pork barrel," projects. These had to be increased for political reasons and strictly "military funds" were already too small to permit significant reductions.

In more ways than one, the chief influence on United States military policy during this decade's remainder was the personality of Franklin D. Roosevelt. The President relished his role as Commander in Chief of the Armed Forces. He often intervened in fundamental questions of military policy. He initially tried to reduce the size of the Regular Officer Corps of the Army to carry through some of his economy programs. Roosevelt's decision to cut the size of the Regular Officer Corps of the Army in 1933 could have had disastrous consequences. On the list of those scheduled to be discharged as "overage in grade" were the now famous names Lucius Clay, Leslie R. Groves, Alfred M. Gruenther, James A. Van Fleet, J. Lawton Collins and Matthew B. Ridgway. Since promotion was strictly by seniority, these officers were first lieutenants after 15 years service through no professional inadequacy. In fact, they had already given promise of the brilliance they were later to display.

Fortunately, this arbitrary slash was blocked by Congress. Ironically, Congressional rejection was inspired by the President's coincident request to call to active duty still larger numbers of Reserve officers to operate the Civilian Conservation Corps project which had been assigned to the Army to administer. The inconsistency of releasing experienced leaders and replacing them with part-time soldiers was obvious. As affairs actually turned out, Roosevelt's creation of the C.C.C. and placing it under Army jurisdiction did much to train thousands of Reserve officers who later proved invaluable in the early days of World War II. In addition, Regular Army personnel gained experience in administration and in handling young men under field conditions—experience which had been impossible in the skeleton-size, economy-ridden Army garrisons. At the same time, the wide participation of the Army Engineers in the public works projects launched by the New Deal familiarized that corps with modern construction techniques.

These were truly days of expediency. As we have since learned, there was no master plan for coping with the depression but many dramatic and imaginative schemes were launched for re-creating enthusiasm and confidence and for coping with the massive unemployment confronting the nation. As the administration swung from economizing to spending its way out of the depression, the Army and Navy hesitantly followed other departments of the government in seeking to spend money quickly in the drive to "buy prosperity" or, at least, to give legitimate work to millions of unemployed. Under this new orientation Army Engineers received what in those days were huge sums to build Fort Peck in Montana, which was then the world's largest earth-fill dam. They were also directed to start obtaining electric power from the strong tidal waters of the Passamaquoddy River in eastern Maine at great expense. Other examples of major engineering undertakings attempted primarily for job inflation was the Florida Ship Canal and the program to make the Missouri River navigable as far as Sioux City, Iowa. The Florida and Passamaquoddy projects were abandoned, after only partial completion, when Congressional investigation revealed the impractability of these bright but unsound suggestions.

At the same time a series of floods brought new ways for the Army to spend money—the elaborate flood controls of the Mississippi, Ohio, and Missouri Rivers carried out by the Army Engineers. On the reverse of this coin, unprecedented drought in the dust bowl states egged civilian departments into extensive expenditures for soil-conservation programs. Meanwhile funds for naval construction permitted the U. S. Fleet, already unbalanced as a result of the Washington Disarmament Conference and government apathy thereafter, to start building its way up to treaty limits. Still another, though relatively insignificant, area of expenditure was funds to make World War I, and even more venerable, military posts more livable. In many military installations today the permanent and beneficial results of New Deal agencies can be seen.

Concurrently with frenzied efforts to spend our way out of the depression, the aggressive designs of Hitler, Mussolini, and Japan became evident. President Roosevelt early saw the implications of the would-be world conquerors and gradually shifted emergency funds for the War and Navy Departments from nonmilitary matters to preparedness. In short, Franklin Roosevelt faced the gradual conversion from peacetime preoccupations to preparation for war much like his Democratic predecessor in office, Woodrow Wilson.

Sights Set Low

Against this shifting political background the acquisition of advanced technology by the Armed Services during the thirties left much to be desired. Many of the same obstacles which we discussed with respect to the twenties carried over to bar adequate exploitation of advanced technologies in our armed forces. World War I equipment was still being used although preserved at nonsensical expense. For example, not until the middle of the decade could the military discard vehicles as worn out even when the cost of annual repairs exceeded their total amortized value! Parenthetically, obsolete practices were forced even more senselessly upon civilian departments. As late as 1939 the U. S. Post Office Department still used 20-year-old trucks. Congressional appropriations forbade the purchase of new vehicles while permitting unlimited repair costs on old ones.

Yet the neglect of technology by the American military could not be entirely attributed to these or other economic reasons. Part of it seemed to be psychological—a pronounced reluctance to venture into new technologies or new ideas. Our military men, of course, preferred better weapons, but cumbersome procedures in development and minimal research facilities confused, if not obscured, their identification and selection. This period might be characterized as one of both opportunities and discouragement. In all fairness, it does not seem that the American armed forces seized every available means to create a modern military force. According to the official history of the Chief of Staff, there was little indication "that the Staff fully utilized such opportunities as came its way."

Equally pertinent is the testimony of Major General Johnson Hagood, himself a member of the General Staff in the years marked by his complaints.[1] General Hagood's eminence in the Army and his long record of achievement warrant attention to his severe postwar judgment that "The fourteen years 1903–17, during which the General Staff had been in existence, had not been spent in making plans for war,

[1] *The Services of Supply*, Johnson Hagood, Houghton Mifflin, 1927.

the purpose for which it was created . . . our unpreparedness did not come from lack of money, lack of soldiers, or lack of supplies. It came from lack of brains, or perhaps it would be best to say, lack of genius . . ."

Although these remarks were written, in 1927, about an earlier period, they apparently retained enough validity in the decade preceding World War II to qualify as a thumbnail sketch of uninspiring military staff performance[2] in that period.

Technology in the Thirties

The First World War drove home to American industry the need for industrial research. Research laboratories of many American corporations owe their existence to that stimulus, born of the handicaps imposed by the sudden loss of German chemical exports because of the British blockade. Yet this industrial advance was not translated into our military hardware during either the twenties or the thirties. William Jennings Bryan's pre-World War I boast that "a million men would spring to arms overnight," though badly tarnished by events, apparently had its counterpart in the American people's ideas regarding industrial mobilization. We continued to take it for granted that a free people, once aroused, could always arm themselves more quickly and ably than any possible enemy, regardless of that enemy's head start.

In hindsight, the verdict of those responsible for our research and development during World War II was that our

[2] *The Chief of Staff, Prewar Plans and Preparations*, Mark S. Watson, Historical Division, Department of the Army, Government Printing Office, 1950, p. 62.

preparations during the thirties were woefully inadequate. Certainly the armed services had not discovered the possibilities of organized research. They did not ask for adequate funds for this specific purpose. But even the military's modest requests were repeatedly reduced before the budget was approved. In short, the responsibility for low appropriations in research and development resides chiefly in the Executive Branch, not the Congress, even though the latter usually pared already slim budget requests to the bone.

At the beginning of the decade, the War and Navy Departments lacked funds to pioneer in improved military equipment much less to venture into far horizons for new weapons. Likewise industry, utterly unaccustomed to research in military fields during times of peace, was no more venturesome in the depression. As an indication of the level of research and development progress in 1932, the War Department reviewed the total of *thirty-four* then existing projects to establish a priority for continued efforts in the event appropriations were further reduced. This small number contrasts with the many thousands of research and development efforts conducted by all the armed forces since the end of the Second World War.

In 1934 a special committee headed by former Secretary of War Newton D. Baker, recommended "that more definite and continuing appropriations should be available for research and development programs." Baker's committee noted that in the past the Bureau of the Budget and Congress had "not considered it advisable . . . to sanction the financial programs" required to implement the work.

Despite this belated recognition of the value of applied military research, within two years the decision was made to actually reduce the research outlay from its $7,000,000 to

$9,000,000 bracket to one of $5,000,000 to $7,000,000 annually. The reason behind this decision to terminate research and development of "unessential" equipment was that "the Army needs large quantities of excellent equipment that has already been developed. The amount of funds allocated to research and development in former years is in excess of the proper proportion for the item in consideration of the rearmament program."[3]

This line of reasoning, however practical it seemed to an Army starved for a minimum of operating equipment, was to be repudiated in a few short years. As soon as the war in Europe began, it became obvious that the U. S. Army's meager equipment appeared obsolete in those fields where military technology had made the greatest progress abroad; especially radar detection of hostile aircraft; fire-control equipment for antiaircraft artillery; armored vehicles, modern anti-tank weapons, and aerial mapping and map reproduction.[4]

American research and development during the early days of World War II revealed how faulty many of the War Department's attitudes and procedures in research and development had been during the thirties. Thus, in mid-1941, General Marshall demanded a revision of "cumbersome peacetime procedures" to be replaced by the most "direct informal contacts between interested individuals."

The know-how to build many of the weapons which were to play a decisive role during World War II existed in the

[3] Memo, AC of S G-4, for C of S, 30 October 1936, sub: Research and Development for FY 1938. Cited in *The Chief of Staff Prewar Plans and Preparations*, p. 42.

[4] Colonel James Bagley of the Corps of Engineers had been an outstanding pioneer in developments of aerial mapping in the 1920s but commercial firms made more use of his discoveries than the military.

thirties. Yet, the actual task of applying this technology to military requirements did not seriously get under way in the United States until mobilizations was forced upon this country by events in Europe. An index of the variety of weapons needed by the Army can be found in the Chief of Staff's inquiries to the heads of the Technical Services in 1939 and 1940. The Chief of Ordnance was asked to report on the development status of land mines, armor piercing and incendiary bombs, fire-control mechanisms, and the use of antiaircraft guns against ground targets. The Chief of Engineers was asked to report on equipment for river crossings, steel pillboxes and methods of exploding enemy land mines. Comment by the Chief of the Air Corps was sought on the status of dive bombers, observation planes, night fighters, and defensive obstructions for airfields. On very few items were the reports encouraging.

The technologies for an effective armored force long antedated World War II. An entire army could have been put on wheels or on tracks, and armor protection provided for infantry. In short, a powerful American army could have been fashioned around the internal-combustion engine, diesel or gasoline, and the caterpillar track. Beyond small experimental units this was not attempted.

Ideas behind the many military applications of rockets go back several centuries. A nineteenth-century British inventor, commenting upon adaptation of an Indian rocket used in siege warfare, termed the rocket "an arm by which the whole system of military tactics has been changed." Rockets were subsequently neglected by all armies for decades only to explode spectacularly on the battlefields of Europe and the cities of Great Britain in World War II. The American bazooka is an example of the short-range rocket which could have easily been perfected in the thirties. Likewise, recoilless rifles, developed in World War II, have origins that can be traced back more than twenty years.

In today's world of intercontinental ballistic missiles it is interesting to note that a Major James R. Randolph, writing in the January 1930 issue of *Ordnance* Magazine, predicted the utilization of rockets for ultralong-range bombardments, theoretically halfway around the globe. He stated that this development would require an efficient, reliable liquid fuel rocket motor of great power. Serious military experimentation on such power sources began not in the United States but in Germany.

Americans discerned the promise of guided missiles at least as early as World War I when the air service tested some embryonic guided flying bombs. This work was largely discontinued during the years between the wars. Again the reason was lack of funds. In 1938 interest was revived, although an industry-wide competition for aerial torpedoes produced unsatisfactory results. By February 1940 the War Department approved a set of specifications for an aerial torpedo which would be capable of striking a target with considerable accuracy. Those paid off handsomely in the ensuing conflict.

Rarely, however, did our effort go into these novel areas of potentially major returns. Instead we hewed the line of marginal improvement. Examples of progress in American artillery are typical. During the First World War the American Army made a field gun for the British. This gun was altered to use 75-mm shells and named the 75-mm gun, model 1917. In 1935, this same model was equipped with rubber tires and, thus improved, moved out to the Philippines. Two weapons used extensively by the American Army in World

War II were the 8-inch howitzer, originally a British design and the 240-mm howitzer, of French design, which we acquired in 1918. Between wars both of these pieces were improved and became the mainstay of our heavier artillery in World War II. But fundamentally, they were basically the same weapons we had acquired from our allies twenty years before. This kind of piecemeal copying, rather than imaginative innovations and invention, set the development tone of the thirties.

Budgetary Strangulation

There have been many efforts made to fix the blame for this slow response to a developing emergency on the Army or on the Bureau of the Budget or on the Congress. The administrative history of the Office of Scientific Research and Development, written in 1948, flatly states that "the initial responsibility for low appropriations for research and development resides in the Executive Branch and not in the Legislative."

Years of penury did indeed seem to have conditioned the reflexes of our military planners. Nevertheless a review of Congressional hearings during the thirties reveals that Army chieftains frequently made direct appeals to Congress for necessary funds. General MacArthur advised the Congress in 1932 that the Army's armored forces "suffer tremendously from one thing and only one thing—that the Congress will not give them enough money to equip them properly with modern tanks." Ordnance Department appropriations requests were repeatedly reduced until in 1934 they barely exceeded $7,000,000 for new equipment. In fact, it can be argued that it was the Navy orders placed with the Army's Ordnance Department during these years that kept the Watertown and Watervliet Arsenals going.

Neither the Army nor the Navy, however, are blameless in their short-sighted expenditure of the limited funds actually made available to them. By the mid-thirties total appropriations for both services were higher than in any previous peacetime period. Yet there were years during the thirties when the Army expended more money for bands and band instruments than it did for Chemical Warfare. Not until 1938 did funds allotted to buy armored vehicles exceed those for horses, mules, harness and wagons. The anachronism of Portée Cavalry—men and horses traveling on highways in huge vans, then mounting for combat—was perpetuated at considerable cost until as late as 1941.

The record shows a rather persistent reluctance to spend money on research and development that would produce significantly new weapons. The official History of the Office of the Chief of Staff is the source of these remarkable statistics:

> . . . Only $5,000,000, 1.2 per cent of the whole military fund and less than four-fifths of a cent in the whole War Department dollar for the year 1939, was allotted to research and development. If this calls for further examination, in perspective, one may observe that $5,000,000 was one-twentieth of the cost of a new battleship which was being laid down by the Navy in that same year. It was one-four-hundredth part of the moneys later to be spent for the research, development, and production of the atomic bomb alone.[5]

[5] C/S PPP, p. 32.

There are other ways of showing that budgetary limitations, wherever imposed, were a rather direct reflection of the low estate in which military research and development was then held. In 1930 the total research and development expenditures for all departments of the U. S. Government was $23,000,000. In 1947 the government expended $625,000,000, exclusive of projects in the atomic energy field. From 1930 to 1952, as attitudes toward national security changed almost as radically, the U. S. Government budget for research and development multiplied some seventy times.

There were other restrictions hampering research not the least of which were the procedures for obligating R&D funds. In 1940, the Chief Army Signal Officer, Major General Joseph O. Mauborgne, stated that if he complied strictly with War Department and Bureau of Budget policy, it would take from one and one-half to two and one-half years to get work started on a new development program. (Unfortunately, versions of this same complaint are often heard today.) Competitive bid contracts were still required, even though obviously incompatible with research needs: the most competent research "supplier" might not be the lowest bidder. The competitive bid requirement was a hangover from Congressional reaction to World War I profiteering when "cost-plus" contracts ran wild.

But research and development is only the first step in the application of technology to military problems. The task of converting industrial plants from the production of civilian goods to military equipment is just as important and even more complicated. Both of the World Wars were essentially wars of matériel. Mass production became an obvious requirement of waging modern war. Successive Industrial

163

Mobilization Plans, drawn up by the Industrial College and the efforts of the Assistant Secretary of War, charged by Congress with preparing for wartime procurement, received no financial support.

Industrial Mobilization

The United States entered the Second World War with the highest level of technological productivity existing in any country. Yet American industry, even as late as 1941, was not prepared to produce military equipment on any large scale. Once the decision was made to mobilize, it became apparent that the arms industries could not be expanded as rapidly as troops could be drafted and trained. Except to the few logistic planners who remembered 1917, this fact of life came as a profound shock to most American officials.

Many important industrial production advances had occurred since 1920. The well-known development of precision measurement and gauging so essential to mass production was a direct offspring of the huge munitions requirements of the first global conflict. One would naturally suppose that, with the advances made by American industrialists in the aftermath of World War I, there would have been no real problems involved in another American mobilization.

The truth was that there were many problems—most of which could have been avoided had authorities heeded the carefully studied, recorded lessons of the previous mobilization which Army planners revised every two years in this prewar decade. As we tried to gear-up for war production, basic shortages and lack of trained industrial workers again appeared all the way across the board, from machine-tool output to basic iron and steel and aluminum production. Again, as in 1917, foreign orders for military equipment, stimulated by Lend-Lease policies, enabled American industrialists to make the changeover faster than would otherwise have been the case. But the salient point remains: American industrial superiority played a small role in constructively influencing U.S. military and foreign policy as the war clouds gathered in the late thirties. In fact, the mere possession of this immense industrial advantage acted as a sedative: we took it for granted that this great asset could be exploited, if necessary, with little or no advance effort.

The sorry state of our industrial preparedness can be seen from a single example—our stock of .30-caliber rifle ammunition. In September 1940, because of shipments to Great Britain following the Dunkirk debacle, the War Department's supply of cartridges totaled only 520,000,000, little more than enough for a normal year's training. This stock left nothing for any expeditionary force or for other emergencies, and, because of the time it would take to accelerate production, no new supplies of importance were expected for a year.

The Army Industrial College, an indirect offshoot of the National Security Act of 1920, proved to be a living link between the Army and those comparatively few industrialists who maintained an interest in military procurement problems. With Navy and Marine officers among its students, the college contributed to bring about Army-Navy co-operation in industrial mobilization—a co-operation which began actually in the early thirties after the Army General Staff reported that the Navy had declined to co-operate in that field.

The War Policies Commission previously cited held

hearings in 1931 at which Army Chief of Staff General MacArthur presented the first industrial mobilization plan, largely the college's work. The dormant Munitions Board was reorganized in 1931 with Assistant Secretary of the War and Navy Departments as members. The following year, the Board took over the sponsorship of the Industrial Mobilization Plan developed at the Army Industrial College. Despite this encouraging assumption of responsibility, the Munitions Board had no legal status nor appropriations until 1939 when it was declared an executive agency and directed to send unresolved matters to the President for decision.

The revived and expanded organization, however, provided a medium in which to harmonize the different service viewpoints regarding mobilization. The Navy, as the first line of defense, a force in being, needed supplies in a high state of readiness for immediate combat operations. The Army, on the other hand, anticipating a huge expansion, sought preparations for the extensive, prompt, and orderly conversion of industries to support the buildup. For this reason the bulk of mobilization planning naturally fell to the Army, but much progress was made in eliminating Army-Navy competition for identical plants and services. Moreover, the early opposition of the Navy's bureau chiefs gradually diminished as they were given representation on the executive committee of the Munitions Board.

Procurement Planning: Army-Navy Co-operation

During the thirties progressive improvements were made in wartime procurement plans based on a growing recognition of the interrelationship between military requirements, business methods, and industrial potential to develop the weapons of war. The Army's original survey, covering more than 20,000 manufacturing establishments, was reduced to less than 10,000 which produced "problem items," a simplification insisted upon by the Navy. Army-Navy agreements thoroughly covered plants in the aircraft, automobile, optical, and precision-instrument industries. Partial coverage was obtained in other fields. Although Navy bureau spokesmen doubted that the allocation system would work, important features of these sweeping plans became fact before the decade's end.

The United States was divided into 14 procurement districts set up to operate on a decentralized basis and thus to avoid the overcentralization which had hampered efforts during World War I. The Army and Navy "divided" industrial plants between them by prior agreement, and the plants thus earmarked were assigned to the Army technical service or Navy Department bureau most directly concerned with the particular kind of production; detailed estimates for requirements were developed for over 4000 items needed in war; wartime procedures for the operation of American railroads were established and accepted by the Association of American Railroads; co-operation was obtained in many sectors of the economy for conducting procurement planning surveys.

Regrettably, these plans reflected no realization of the need for such provisions as a controlled materials plan or expediting research in synthetic rubber both of which became major tasks early in the war. Lists of personnel, however, were forehandedly drawn up to staff the wartime government procurement agencies, and some of these personnel were selected for Reserve officer commissions. The War Department G-3 wisely suggested in 1932 that the public be informed of these provisions but was turned down on the grounds that there was "no provision for peacetime advertising by the War Department."

The 1933 edition of the mobilization plan was reviewed by the Senate Committee investigating the munitions industry, chaired by Senator Gerald P. Nye of North Dakota, and with Alger Hiss as staff director. Actually, the Nye Committee stated that the plan was weak in "provisions to prevent profiteering" and "to protect labor" but gave the War Department broad general support for the plan. The critical report of the Nye Committee contained constructive elements that a wiser nation might have heeded. That committee found that despite years of planning neither the Army nor the Navy possessed reliable cost data, nor did they have adequate information upon which to "shrewdly evaluate industrial costs."[6] These deficiencies had wasted public funds in World War I and delayed production. To a lesser, but still harmful degree, these shortcomings were soon to be repeated.

The Navy's full participation in the 1936 Mobilization Plan was a heartening sign of growing Army-Navy co-operation in industrial liaison. Also the reluctance of the military to bestow wartime emergency powers on already existing agencies of the civil government gradually diminished. Nevertheless areas of friction remained. The 1936 Mobilization Plan aroused the ire of the Army General Staff by including an appendix on selective service and public relations which the General Staff regarded as its own province.

[6] Pendleton Herring, The Impact of War, Farrar and Rinehart, 1941, p. 197.

As the decade neared its end, the impact of events in Europe slightly loosened the purse strings. Two million dollars was allotted in 1938 to initiate the long-sought educational orders with industry. The next year, over thirty-four million dollars was applied to educational orders. In addition, a three-year program to spend $100,000,000 to stockpile strategic materials, one of the repeated recommendations of previous Industrial Mobilization Plans, began in 1939—with a modest $10,000,000 appropriation. Implementation of this program required a rapid increase in the procurement staffs of the technical services. This kind of realistic progress continued in the preparation of the 1939 plan, although it is worthy of note that the State Department killed the War Department recommendation to send officers to London to study mobilization developments in Europe. As a substitute, questionnaires were sent out to military attachés who, unfortunately in this respect, were usually selected for traditional combat qualifications rather than for industrial and procurement experience.

Looking back, the military deserves a great deal of credit for its foresighted attempts in mobilization planning. In fact, most of the provisions of their mobilization plans were acted upon on a piecemeal basis during World War II. On the negative side, our unreadiness for industrial mobilization was underscored by the need to completely reorganize Army logistics at the war's start.

Despite its merits, the Mobilization Plan proposed such far-reaching controls over the civilian economy as to be politically unacceptable in time of peace. The President rejected the final prewar version of 1939 on the grounds that it over emphasized military control at the expense of civilian participation. As often happens, the attacks against specific features of the plan, many of them unfounded, received far greater publicity than the contents of the plan itself, which were never understood by the public. Some of the opposition was semantic. The use of terms, like "war planning" and "war resources," implied another dreadful conflict. Large segments of public opinion still echoed the peace-at-any-price sentiments of their 1914–17 spiritual forebears. The simple substitution of the word "defense" instead of "war" might have had significant effect. In short, the War Department fumbled its public relations.

Several basic philosophical reasons lay beneath the public rejection of the 1939 plan. All were related to the fact that our society will not sacrifice individual pursuits to the common good until danger is imminent and obvious. For example, why should any automobile manufacturer attempt to make tanks at a low profit when he could, up to 1941, manufacture automobiles at a big profit? Consequently, one of the main disputes in 1941, prior to Pearl Harbor, was whether or not to cancel or curtail civilian auto production. Action was not taken until after Pearl Harbor, which leads us to another basic question: Is a free enterprise system willing to meet the demanding needs of national security with profit and income incentives below those generally considered desirable in time of peace?

Military Progress: Amphibious Warfare and Tanks

Largely neglected in the headlines of the thirties, military developments already in progress were to have a major influence in shaping the outcome of the Second World War. The revolution in transportation that has epitomized this century was to be accelerated during the early 1940s. Advances in both airplane and automotive transportation were to give a new meaning to mobility. Similarly, the ability to hurl projectiles over distant space was to be immensely increased. Orthodox artillery during World War II was to achieve ranges six times greater than artillery could muster in 1900. The German V-1, prototype of today's guided missile and drawing upon Dr. Goddard's original research, raised the range to well over 200 miles. And if the airplane is regarded as a long range projectile carrier, there was almost no limit.

Amphibious warfare doctrine evolved very early in the interwar period. It sprouted from prophetic plans, developed by Lieutenant Colonel Earl H. Ellis, USMC, in 1921. These plans provided for fleet bases, stretching westward from Pearl Harbor to Samoa, through which the U.S. might project its naval power as far as the Philippines. Ellis recognized that the reconquest of any Pacific island bases taken by Japan would require amphibious counterattack across well-defended beaches. This realistic insistence created a demand for amphibious forces. Eventually a group of Marines perceived that the Corps' future rested in its continued development as such a force. By 1934, the basic doctrine of amphibious warfare was developed and withstood prolonged tests and trial without fundamental change. For a variety of reasons, however, the 1934 doctrine was not implemented with adequate techniques before 1942.

Ultimately, developments in naval design were to make possible amphibious landings on remote shores against a strongly entrenched enemy. Such craft, up to but not including LSTs, were long known, but no one in top authority was genuinely interested in their development. Even after

Pearl Harbor the Navy seemed reluctant to invest in equipment for amphibious warfare sufficient for more than a limited number of Marine Corps landing teams. This reluctance stemmed from a shortage of steel and a critical priorities problem of allocating between carriers, battleships, submarines, and landing craft the steel made available to the Navy. Surprisingly the first large-scale training in the use of landing craft by U.S. amphibious units was undertaken by the Army Engineers on Cape Cod in the spring of 1942 while arguments concerning priorities in the naval building program raged inside the Navy Department.

The problem of training personnel for amphibious warfare was a complicated one. The Navy was unable to train crews for shore-to-shore operations on the scale required for the expected landings in the European Theatre of Operations as long as it stuck to its policy of voluntary enlistments. Under this policy the Navy could obtain necessary personnel only for ship-to-shore operations in the Pacific area. A joint United States strategic committee decided, therefore, to separate this training into two major areas. The marines assumed responsibility for ship-to-shore training on island attacks in the Pacific, while the Army carried on training preparations for shore-to-shore operations in the European theater. This division of responsibility was made early in 1942.

The Engineer Amphibious Command opened its training program at Camp Edwards, Massachusetts, on June 10, 1942. It was located nearby the amphibious training center of the Army Ground Forces. The Engineers were compelled to take on what would normally have been the Navy's beach party and the Marine Corps' shore party tasks. "Engineer Brigades" with shore regiments and boat regiments evolved in 1943 as an answer to these requirements. Subsequently the war-born Transportation Corps was able to assume this capability and relieve the Corps of Engineers from the problems confronting "white water" sailors. This brief record of events in no way detracts from the pioneer work of the Marine Corps in developing amphibious doctrine and techniques. A tribute should be paid here to a military group which logically progressed from doctrinal theory to laboratory tests and thence to the weapons and techniques which made the doctrine valuable.

The 1931 revision of the (1920) National Defense Act's provision which had tied tanks inseparably to the infantry permitted the painfully slow birth of an Armored Corps in this country. That revision was largely the work of Dwight F. Davis, Secretary of War in the Coolidge administration, whose enthusiasm had been kindled by an effective demonstration of armored vehicles during English army maneuvers. But funds for the promotion of a distinct armored corps were doled out so parsimoniously that it was five years before a "mechanized brigade of cavalry" (two regiments of "fast" tanks) were organized, at Fort Knox, Kentucky.

The infantry continued to develop "close support tanks," and the U.S. fought World War II with the dual program: armored divisions to exploit breakthroughs, and separate tank battalions to rumble alongside infantry. Tank destroyer units were formed late in the decade to fill a tactical void since U.S. armor doctrine counseled against tank clashes with hostile armor. The tank-destroyer concept of fast but essentially armorless gun platforms did not hold up too well in combat.

On the other side of the ocean, lack of money plus official indifference prevented British armored formations from achieving their maximum prewar potential. But the foresight of a small group of officers, including Major General J. F. C. Fuller, achieved continuous improvement in quality of material and tactics.

Naval Technological Pace

Shifting from land to sea one can follow the steady plan of naval warfare techniques. The Navy was the first military service to experience technological change at so fast a pace that doctrine, tactics, and training often lagged behind inventiveness and construction. The period of the thirties witnessed a progressive improvement in naval technology in many areas of sea warfare. The most notable advances were doubtless in antisubmarine operations and in the perfection of the fleet Air Arm, but considerable progress was made in battleship design. Qualitative improvement in battleships was effected by giving them greater speed, stronger armor protection and superior fire control and comprehensive antiaircraft defenses (although these last were insufficiently appreciated until Pearl Harbor). In the field of logistic support, development of the high-speed naval tanker and refueling techniques at sea were to make possible the long operational cruises involved in the Navy's campaigns in the Pacific in World War II. Similarly, great advances in radio communication made possible the control of fleet operations over the wide stretches of ocean.

The Navy likewise coped successfully with the welter of technological problems required in forging the world's most effective naval air striking force. The techniques of carrier flying had to be developed, crews trained and the tactics for projecting carrier planes into offensive warfare developed. These tactics were not completed fully until World War II was under way. The crucial factor, of course, was the development of planes appropriate to naval warfare. Here the Navy had to face up to the dilemma of mass producing a given model too soon or be lacking in combat readiness if an emergency arose prior to perfecting a given plane. On the whole the Navy decided to delay purchasing planes in large orders until the aircraft industry could produce carrier aircraft capable of the job but susceptible to improvement. Concurrent with the development of naval aircraft was the growth of the carrier itself. After 1936, that aircraft design had progressed far enough to justify the steady building program of modern carriers to team up with the older *Lexington* and *Saratoga*.

Submarine detection technology was one field in which the U.S. forged ahead, as noted by the report of the 1938 Hepburn Board on the status of U.S. sea power. Sound navigation and ranging (sonar) had passed operational tests in 1933, replacing ASDIC (Allied Submarine Devices Investigating Committee) developed by the British in World War I. *Sound* ranging is superior to early *echo* ranging since it permits longer ranges—less affected by noises of the originating ship.

Working without authorized funds, the Navy had wangled submarine detection tests at sea and attained an effective range of 1200 yards as early as 1930. By 1937, in association with the Woods Hole Oceanographic Institute, Navy units were conducting operational research in the Caribbean. This work became the foundation for the war program of ASWORG (Antisubmarine Warfare Operations Research

Group), a part of the famous "Tenth Fleet," a secret naval research organization.

On the debit side, however, stands the deplorable performance of the torpedoes with which our submarines were equipped when war began. Fundamental deficiencies in these weapons were not corrected until well into 1943. Part of the trouble stemmed from prewar prohibitions against using expensive live torpedoes for tests.

Air Power's Rise

In this decade, the one area in which technology decisively influenced military policy was that of aviation. Personal experience and analysis of the 1917–18 campaigns had convinced many aviators that airplane development called for a basic reappraisal of traditional military doctrine and strategy. The U.S. contingent of these air enthusiasts, whose chief spokesman had been General Mitchell, was convinced that the Army and the Navy, either through lack of knowledge or imagination, had utterly failed to appreciate the full combat value of this new weapon (see Chapter IV). The passage of years and technological advance, rather than any decisions emanating from the continuing doctrinal disputes, finally settled the issue.

This controversy, which would have been slow to resolve on any basis, was exacerbated by lack of development funds. For the first six years of post-Versailles peace, the Army Air Corps' annual appropriation was never higher than $16,000,000. Nevertheless, because many aviation adherents recognized that their case depended upon increased performance in aircraft, a relatively large percentage of that small budget was allocated to research and development. This trend began early. In 1924, for example, the Air Service had allocated nearly 25 per cent of its total appropriation, other than pay of military personnel, to research and development.

In 1926 the Air Corps established its chief center for research, engineering, and testing activities at Wright Field near Dayton, Ohio, which was destined to play a major role in the growth of American air power. It is interesting to note, in terms of present-day research efforts, that the total investment in experimental facilities at Wright Field by 1939 amounted to some $10,000,000.

Fortunately, the Air Service did not have to depend entirely upon its own resources. Together with other agencies of the government it made considerable use of the National Advisory Council for Aeronautics which, as previously mentioned, Congress had established in 1915 to undertake "scientific research on the fundamental problems of flight." Furthermore, the Air Corps, beginning in 1926, laid down a policy which permitted its contractors to amortize an experimental development from the income derived from subsequent production contracts. Under this policy funds actually devoted to research and development were effectively higher than those specifically accounted for in the budget, and, perhaps more significant, private industry was motivated to undertake additional research.

The military policy problem raised by the earliest debates over air power was basically then, as now, a question of national strategy. How would aeronautical development affect America's geopolitical position? Could we continue to remain aloof from the rest of the world, safe within the ramparts of the Western Hemisphere, or would we become more and more involved in the disputes of Europe and Asia?

Further, if involved, would we be able to pursue an essentially defensive strategy, or would the growing capabilities of air power impose upon us an offensive military posture? This fundamental issue hovered behind the numerous governmental investigations into the role of air power in the United States during the two decades following World War I.

As early as 1928, Major General Mason M. Patrick, recently retired Chief of the Air Corps, wrote: "The air effort of the United States since we entered the World War has probably been the most investigated activity ever carried on by the United States." Investigations into the status and program of United States air power continued. Yet the thirties, stamped as they were by neutrality, pacifism, the depression, and the bitterly conflicting partisan spirits aroused by the New Deal, clouded an objective assessment of air power in relation to our over-all military problems.

The ostensible issues on which the debate was conducted were clear enough. Air power enthusiasts believed that the potentialities of the new weapon called for a drastic revamping of the national defense structure. The leaders of both the Army and Navy, however, continued to hold that the airplane's principal duty was to give immediate support to ground forces and surface fleets in the furtherance of their traditional missions.

In defense of the admirals and the Army generals, it should be pointed out that their basic responsibility was for the current defense of the United States. The potentialities claimed for air power still did not emerge clearly in the mid-thirties. Although rapid technological improvements in aviation had occurred since the First World War, Mitchell's impassioned pleas for massed bomber formations during that conflict and Italy's General Giulio Douhet's more expansive claims shortly after remained theoretical arguments, not substantiated under existing "state of the art."

Technical limitations stood in the way. The comparatively short ranges, the influence of weather on flight, the necessity for numerous bases, continued mechanical unreliability and the speed with which obsolescence overtook production's output jutted into the path of developing air power's full potential. Looking back, the disputes concerning air power seem to lie between one group of people whose ideas consistently outpaced technological developments and another group whose outlook was anchored to demonstrated achievements rather than to potential growth.

The Birth of Big Bombers

By 1930 the science of aeronautics had reached the stage which made relatively big long-range bombing planes a possibility. Thereafter the policy issue hinged more clearly on the Air Corps' technological success in making the long-range bomber a reality. The B-17, whose genesis can be traced back to 1933, became in a direct sense the demonstration piece of modern American air power.

That year, the Air Corps announced a design competition for a multi-engine long-range bomber. The Boeing Aircraft Company entered this competition with a four-engine bomber of revolutionary design. In July 1935, the prototype of the B-17 made its first test flight. It should be noted that the frequently castigated General Staff encouraged the development of this bomber by approving its military characteristics in 1934. It justified these characteristics by assigning a technical mission to the Air Force for "the destruction by bombs of distant land or naval targets" and the ability "to reinforce Hawaii, Panama, and Alaska without the use of intermediate facilities." Not only did the War Department support the action leading to the development of the B-17, but it gave approval in 1935 (later temporarily withdrawn) for an even larger experimental bomber which resulted, eventually, in the B-29, so important in the far reaches of the Pacific war. The B-29 was the first aircraft to deliver an atomic bomb.

General Henry H. Arnold, Commanding General of the U. S. Army Air Force in World War II, pointed to the year 1935 as the turning point in the history of air power. In that year the B-17 bomber was first produced in the United States, and the Manchester bomber was manufactured in England. As General Arnold stated, the Royal Air Force "had its own Ministry, its own uniform . . . its own budget, but only with the development of the Manchester bomber did it begin to acquire striking power."

The first delivery of the B-17 to an operational unit came in 1937, four years of lead time after the plane's original design had been drafted. This long lead-time period, destined to elongate with the increasing complexity of successive aircraft and weapons, provides a striking example of the military problems inherent in technological change, problems of continuously increasing influence on military planning and strategy.

From the mid-thirties onward the Air Corps was increasingly beset by serious lead-time problems. The Army Air Force fought World War II with aircraft which had either been in production or under development prior to December 7, 1941. Despite intensive efforts during the war, lead time was never less than three and often as much as five years. Jet propulsion, the major wartime achievement in research and development, did not reach maturity until after the war was over. But while the Air Force fought with prewar types of planes, constant modifications made the 1945 versions far superior to their '41 and '42 predecessors.

Two developments of the thirties, the supercharger and the controlled-pitch, constant-speed propeller, greatly increased the efficiency of the aircraft engine and helped make possible the goals of air power enthusiasts. The controlled-pitch, constant-speed propeller could be set to maintain any chosen engine speed and thereby assure maximum utilization of available engine power under all conditions. The supercharger was used to compensate for the lower density of air at high altitudes by bringing a constant amount of oxygen into the combustion chamber.

The development of the B-17 confirmed the views of Army airmen that the future role of the Air Corps lay in "long-range strategic operations." Yet this viewpoint clashed with the prevailing temper of isolationism and neutralism. Air power's claims for a decisive role in strategy were still limited technologically. That the Air Corps itself recognized these limitations may be found in a study, "The Functions of the Army Air Forces," presented by the Air Corps Board on October 29, 1936. Assuming that, with current performance of aircraft, sustained attacks could *not* be carried out against the territory of any major foreign power from bases inside the U.S., the board declared that the Air Corps' immediate and primary concern should be with national defense. Until an adequate defense was assured, "the diversion of effort incident to preparations for strategically offensive operations is not justified."

Thus, it is not surprising that the B-17, when received by

the GHQ, Air Force, in 1937, was described as an ideal weapon for coastal defense. In the mood of the thirties it was difficult to offer justification for the long-range bomber on any other grounds.

At this time, the Chief of Staff gave the following directions to the Air Corps: "Experimentation in research will be confined to types of aircraft for the close support of ground troops. No funds to be set up for the development of the heavy-bomber types."

In 1938 a program for acquiring long-range bombers was sent back to the Air Corps with a policy admonition:

"(1) Our national policy contemplates preparation for defense, not aggression, (2) Defense of sea areas, other than within the coastal zone, is a function of the Navy, (3) The Military superiority of . . . a B-17 over the two or three smaller planes that could be procured with the same funds remains to be established, in view of the vulnerability, air-base limitation and complexity in operation of the former type . . . If the equipment to be provided for the Air Corps be that best adapted to carry out the specific functions appropriately assigned it under Joint Action . . . there would appear to be no need for a plane larger than the B-17."[7]

This action temporarily reversed the decision to build the B-29 and slowed down procurement of B-17s. As General Arnold wrote later: "Had we had the 1000 B-17s in 1939 we had requested, the President of the U.S.A. could have prevented the European War"—not too much of an exaggeration.

[7] Mark S. Watson, *Chief of Staff, Prewar Plans and Preparations*, pp. 35 and 36.

The Navy Builds Its Wings

Meanwhile, the Navy's strong interest in building up its fleet Air Arm grew at an increasing pace. The mutual insulation of Army and Navy aviation, however, fostered divergent tactical doctrines. Army Air Corps spokesmen followed watered-down versions of Mitchell-Douhet in proclaiming the strategic unity of air power, whether land- or sea-based, and persistently opposed employment "in penny packets" for direct support of surface action. Naval aviation had, in its own eyes, found its justification in the carrier striking force first unveiled in the 1929 maneuvers that featured a simulated attack against the Panama Canal. Neither group gave serious attention to a mission destined to figure strongly in World War II operations, namely antisubmarine operations by aircraft.

It was in the middle of this decade, also, that the government canceled airmail contracts and assigned to the Army Air Corps the thankless task of flying the mail routes. These measures jolted aviation development. The accompanying "punitive action" against the aircraft industry "all but stopped progress" in commercial aviation.[8]

Nonetheless, American commercial aviation during the thirties excelled over military aviation in some respects. Regular transocean passenger air service was a U.S. first. A Pan American Clipper, U.S. built, blazed a trail over the Pacific in 1935, and over the Atlantic in 1939. Catalina flying boats originally built in the thirties became work horses of Navy air patrols in World War II. But again, the benefits of

[8] E. E. Wilson, *Wings of the Dawn*, p. 73.

these feats of commercial aviation were largely withheld from its military counterpart.

The Navy did receive some support, however, for its pet project of fleet carrier aviation. The *Ranger*, first U.S. naval vessel designed and constructed as a carrier, was commissioned in 1934. The *Yorktown* followed three years later, and the *Enterprise* in May 1938. The carrier *Wasp* was not placed in service until April 1940, and the first escort carrier, the USS *Long Island*, evidence of a long-overdue attention to the problems of antisubmarine warfare, was commissioned in June 1941. Simultaneously, development of carrier aircraft increased the combat capability of naval air power.

A parallel effort by the Army Air Corps to expand its long-range bomber strength met a stern rebuff in May 1938. As previously noted, the Army's Deputy Chief of Staff chided Air Corps planners, stating that the B-17 was the limit in size.[9] A few weeks later Secretary of War Harry H. Woodring instructed the Chief of the Air Corps that estimates for bombers would be restricted to "light, medium, and attack types."[10] Not until September 1939, when news of the Nazi blitzkrieg into Poland crowded the headlines, did the Air Board (of the Air Corps) authoritatively advise the War Department of the urgent need for long-range air operations over both land and sea.

President Roosevelt took a personal interest in the development of the aircraft industry after listening to Hitler's Nuremberg speech on September 12, 1938. Harry Hopkins was dispatched to the West Coast to prepare an estimate of the possibilities for expanding aircraft production. On Octo-

[9] Mark S. Watson, *Chief of Staff, Prewar Plans and Preparations*, p. 35.
[10] Ibid.

ber 26, the President used the occasion of the Herald Trib-
une Forum in New York to warn that "neither we, nor any
nation, will accept disarmament while neighbor nations are
armed to the teeth." By the time the annual budget was
prepared for submission to Congress in January 1939, the
President had decided upon a 6000-plane Air Corps expansion program. In a special message to Congress in January
1939, the President stated: "the Baker Board report of a
few years ago is completely out of date." He elaborated that
"increased range, increased speed, increased capacity of airplanes abroad, have changed our requirements for defensive
aviation."

Again it was the German blitzkrieg in the spring of 1940
which gave the development of air power its final push. General Arnold was allotted $1,500,000,000 and told "to get an
Air Force." The President who had talked of 10–20,000
planes in 1938 began to speak of an output at the rate of
50,000 per year. In the twelve months beginning July 1940,
the Air Corps was to put more than $100,000,000 into re-
search alone, including $42,000,000 for testing the very
heavy bombers for which in 1938 the General Staff had foreseen no need whatever.

In retrospect, not until the gathering storm in Europe and
Asia darkened our horizons and dislodged some deep-rooted
political prejudices and inhibitions could our nascent air
power capitalize on the technological achievements of airplane designers and manufacturers. The important point,
however, is that there was a doctrine of air power, imperfectly
though it was conceived, which drew from an advanced technology the assurance that its promises could be fulfilled.
Hence, technological achievements in aviation had a direct

influence on the evolution of American military policy during the thirties, in distinct contrast to the negligible influence of technology upon other military areas during the same period.

Science and the Military

Any objective appraisal of World War II will reveal how much the victory was owed to those scientists who matched their wits with the enemy in the design of new weapons for war. Prior to that conflict industry had financed the bulk of scientific research in this country, and almost all of this research was devoted to civilian uses.

Scientific collaboration with the government in time of war has a long history in this country. The National Academy of Sciences was chartered during the Civil War for the express purpose of making available to the government the help of civilian scientists. During World War I, the National Research Council was organized to supplement the National Academy in making available scientific research to the nation. Unfortunately, little of this kind of collaboration took place during the thirties. In 1937, for example, the Presidential National Resources Commission, reporting on technological trends and national policy, recommended that a series of studies be undertaken on the following inventions: "mechanical cotton picker, air conditioning, plastics, photoelectric cell, artificial fibers, synthetic rubber, prefabricated houses, television, gasoline production from coal, steepflight aircraft, and tray agriculture (hydroponics)."

It is noteworthy that not a single invention of immediate military import except perhaps the steepflight aircraft was considered worthy of special effort by the scientists on this committee. Barely three years later, the National Research Defense Committee was formed to aid the Army and Navy in carrying out research on military devices. The scope of this activity was expanded in 1941 by the creation of the Office for Scientific Research and Development with power to initiate research as well as to carry out research projects conceived by the military.

Again, as in other aspects of this investigation, the preparatory role that scientists actually played in the development of advanced military techniques fell far short of its potential, later demonstrated vividly under the duress of battle. This in no sense disparages the great achievements of American scientists in World War II. It does reveal, however, that American scientists, like many of their colleagues in other professions during the thirties, were neglectful to the point of imperviousness to the technical problems of national security. Even so, the development of the atomic bomb suggests that American science awakened sooner than others. Albert Einstein's personal letter to President Roosevelt after the Navy's rebuff of Enrico Fermi must be reckoned one of the most portentous events of World War II.

This country had the capability of developing during the thirties many of the weapons which materially influenced victory in World War II. All the basic technical knowledge required for their design and construction was available within the United States. Many of these advances were reflected in revolutionary new machines and equipment throughout our civilian economy. Lacking was recognition of the need to direct some of our technological and scientific skill to the problems of military security. We ignored the lessons of Russian and German experience in the "laboratory" of the Spanish Civil War. Looking back, it is hard to find a single culprit. If the military were overly conservative, the scientists were disinterested. Greater apathy was evident in the public, the Congress, and the administration.

Problems and Policy

To sum up: The technological potential of the thirties was scarcely tapped by our military services, except in the field of aviation. The Air Arms of the Army and the Navy each made tremendous advances, but the entrenched conservatism of the established Services robbed both of optimum improvement.

In reviewing the record of the thirties, the shortcomings of our military leaders should be viewed with a certain amount of charity. General MacArthur, as Chief of Staff, dramatized the leadership problem in 1934, when the Army was running the CCC camps: "in many cases there is but one officer on duty with an entire battalion; this lack of officers has brought Regular Army training in the continental United States to a virtual standstill. . . . Stocks and matériel," he continued, "were inadequate even for limited forces . . . and, such as they are, manifestly obsolescent. The secrets of our weakness are secrets only to our own people." As late as 1939 American armed forces, although rising from their virtual prostration of 1933, were still weak in numbers and ill-equipped in comparison with the standards of their potential enemies. Soldiers trained with "simulated equipment": wooden mockups served as antitank guns; trucks carried placards labeled TANK.

Each of the armed services had its special problems, but the one operating under the greatest restrictions was doubtless the U. S. Army Air Corps, predecessor of the present Air Force. In the light of such restrictions, the expansion of U. S. Army air power from an organization with fewer men than the Field Artillery in 1939 to an autonomous military Service by 1947 was a powerful achievement. The growth of Air Force research and development funds is particularly striking: they were to burgeon from some $7,500,000 in 1939 to one hundred times that sum in 1956.

Requirements of the military establishment in the prewar decade had negligible influence on national policy. There was insignificant connection between domestic programs and military security.

The period of the thirties was studded with investigations as to the causes of war and proposed panaceas for the preservation of peace. The numerous inquiries into the causes of war were all "framed in historical settings, contained no hint of radical changes in warfare."[11]

During this decade a Constitutional amendment was proposed in the United States Senate to make "war for any purpose illegal." War was to be declared only after popular vote. A Congress that could seriously entertain such a pious but pernicious Utopia could scarcely be expected to provide for an adequate defense establishment.

As might be expected, public disparagement of such inadequate military forces as managed to exist was rife among the "intellectuals." Historians Charles A. and Mary R. Beard wrote in *America in Midpassage*:[12] "The Army and Navy expressed foreign as well as domestic policy, wittingly

[11] Pendleton Herring, *The Impact of War*, Farrar and Rinehart, 1941, p. 196.

[12] The Macmillan Company, 1939.

or not . . . influenced by the historic dark urge to war." So, too, domestic politics had their share in stunting technological growth. Increased tariffs restricted foreign imports, freeing industry from any necessity to compete with improved products of overseas industry.

Any sagacious observer perceived in the years after 1935 the certain harbingers of the coming conflict. Yet America's leaders, even those sensitive to the approaching storm, did little to exploit the potential power of the United States either to avert or shorten the conflict.

From 1933 to 1939 Germany allocated an average 10 per cent of her gross national product to military preparedness. "Though prostrate in 1932, Germany became the greatest military power in Europe by 1938. The United States in the late 1920s produced more than the other six great powers combined, yet American influence in world politics was far from commensurate. Huge economic strength had no counterpart willingness to put it in any appreciable degree to military use."[13]

In the words of another observer: "As a powerful military state, we might readily have forced potential aggressor nations to keep the peace. As a country ready to make economic concessions implicit in persuading other nations to disarm and co-operate internationally, we might have stabilized trade and moved to genuine collective security. We did neither."[14]

Soon, events were to pass judgments on our omissions.

[13] Klaus Knorr, *War Potential of Nations*, Princeton University Press, 1956, p. 59.

[14] Pendleton Herring, *The Impact of War*, Farrar and Rinehart, 1941, p. 205.

CHAPTER VI

TECHNOLOGY'S WAR-BORN SURGE

NO ANALYSIS OF AMERICA'S MILITARY-INDUSTRIAL POSITION can be meaningful without a brief look at the continued impact of the Second World War on our technological fortunes. The difficult process of rousing and rearming the American nation during its last major conflict has been described at length by others.[1] We are here concerned solely with the long-range impact of that war on the level, scope, and direction of our subsequent efforts to put technology to work in the defense of the Free World.

American scientists facilitated the technological breakthroughs of World War II, a war that witnessed a virtual revolution in weapons development and improvement. The accumulated scientific knowledge of the past twenty years was exploited more systematically than ever before. American scientists were instrumental in the creation of the Office of Scientific Research and Development which became a

[1] Noteworthy are Mark S. Watson's *Chief of Staff, Prewar Plans and Preparations* and Donald M. Nelson's *Arsenal of Democracy* which examine the complex interactions of military requirements and the civilian economy, the former from the military viewpoint, the latter from that of industry.

synonym of technological boldness and imagination. The war dramatically ended a two-decade hiatus. Both in the development of new weapons and the unprecedented production of arms, the United States became the "arsenal of democracy" in fact as well as in metaphor.

The reasons for our "miracle of mobilization" were not hard to find. American industry, in its peaceful pursuits, had already learned to meld hundreds and thousands of specific research, design, and engineering task into the gigantic enterprises represented by our largest corporations. When war came, American industry was ready to put this know-how to the service of the nation at large.

The United States, in 1939, had by far the largest industrial output of any nation. Its industrial processes outclassed those of any rival. The animus of competition had vested its industrial system with a unique dynamism, particularly in those areas to be converted to war production. In addition, the United States' industrial capability covered the entire spectrum of industries essential for a comprehensive military technology. Nothing was lacking on which to build. Even national shortages in raw materials were often eliminated by the combined efforts of science and industry as in the perfection of synthetic rubber. The basic elements of American technology were linked by the sinews of the most complex and modern transportation and communication system ever devised.

The civilian economy boasted generally good and sometimes outstanding facilities for research and development, usually associated with the major corporations, covering a wide range of investigation. Many large companies, such as the Ford Motor Company, had a completely integrated system of production from raw materials to finished products.

As we entered into the war, a sizable pool of unemployed engineers was available to staff a large-scale military development program.

To summarize: All the ingredients of a first-class military technology existed in the United States at the outbreak of World War II, including highly skilled technical personnel, facilities for basic and applied research, research centers in universities and in industry and the industrial-engineering capacity to turn ideas into equipment. All that was lacking was governmental decision to mobilize these capabilities in behalf of national security. The government, which prior to 1939 had done pitifully little to encourage our free enterprise system to devote some of its vast energies to national defense, initiated under the urgency of war a major reorientation of our economy. A permanent mobilization of an important segment of America's productivity came into being—a mobilization which set the stage for technology's new and demanding role in the dawning nuclear age.

Allies Contribute to American Defense

The contribution of American science during World War II is a matter of record. The triumphs attained, however, were primarily in the application of basic research to military hardware, rather than in the discovery of fundamentally new scientific concepts. Even the success of the Manhattan Project rested on discoveries and theories mostly attributable to European scientists in the years and decades before. It is highly unlikely that any discoveries in basic science made later than 1935 could have been translated into military applications during the course of World War II, even had such discoveries been made.

As we moved into World War II we were again able to reap the technological harvest that had been planted by others. Fortunately for this country, the British generally executed their responsibility to military research and development with foresight despite the resistance of the R.A.F.'s "bomber clique" to air defense measures. The irreplaceable fighters and radar that won the Battle of Britain originated in research supported by private aircraft companies in the mid-thirties. Two U. S. Navy physicists had discovered the principles of what we now call radar in 1925. The discovery languished for ten years in the files of the Naval Research Laboratory until it came to the attention of the Superintendent of the Radio Department of the National Physical Laboratory in Britain. Robert A. Watson-Watt, who was to be knighted for his achievements in radar, turned this American scientific discovery into one of the most spectacular components of the Allies' arsenal in World War II. Had British scientists delayed the start of their radar developments, the outcome of the Battle of Britain might have been quite different.

Shortly after the British work began, Colonel William R. Blair, Signal Corps, initiated a parallel developmental radar at Fort Monmouth, New Jersey. A workable set was demonstrated to the Secretary of War early in 1937. Industrial construction of two different types of radar sets, one for early warning and another for antiaircraft artillery control, soon followed. Hawaii[2] and Panama received the first com-

---

[2] This radar detected Japanese aircraft approaching on the morning of Dec. 7, 1941. Why they were not *identified* as hostile is partly the story of Pearl Harbor, partly the problem of integrating new technologies into active military operation.

pleted sets in 1941. The patent for these sets was not made public until 1957.

Radar—in the sense of a usable, nonvisual detection and fire-control system—drew upon a multitude of inventions. Its full development required reorganization across technical services and combat arms; changing the design of aircraft; revamping the structure of the armed forces—our own as well as those of our British ally. Radar necessitated information centers, communications networks, gun control, and aircraft flight control, all coherently meshed. The British took the lead in these developments.

British foresight is also evident in other areas. When World War II began, the British Army was the only one in Europe which had entirely adopted motor transport and permanently retired the horse to pasture. The U. S. Army benefitted from British innovations in tanks and armored guns as soon as our war-born collaboration began.

The records regarding explosives also underscore United States indebtedness to British research. Before World War II was over, RDX, one and one-half times as powerful as TNT by weight and nearly twice as powerful by volume, was extensively used by our forces. U. S. Ordnance had examined RDX after World War I and rejected it as less stable than other propellents. The British, attracted by its promise, experimented to produce a stable mixture which could be handled without hazard. American and British scientists and engineers, working together, were able during the war to work out a safe and cheap means of quantity production.

A significant surprise weapon of World War II was the so-called VT or proximity fuse. This fuse, activated by reflected radio waves, would explode a shell or a bomb at a pre-set distance from a target. Although ultimately produced in this country, the fuse was made possible by the early research of British and Canadian scientists. Shells armed with VT fuses and fired only over water, to prevent "duds" from imparting the secret to our Axis foes, accounted for the unique accuracy of American AA guns in the Pacific. Unveiled for battlefield use in the Ardennes, December 1944, they materially aided in flattening the Bulge.

British achievements in perfecting the famous Spitfire fighter planes which performed so effectively in the Battle of Britain are well known. The Swedish Bofors light antiaircraft guns, top performers against low-flying planes during World War II, were introduced to this country in 1941 via the British. All armies experimented with quick-erection, demountable bridges, but the British "Bailey" completely outclasssed all others, being adopted by our Army overseas before the War Department could be convinced of its merit. Only in the field of floating (pontoon) bridges did United States experimentation excel. The American Treadway bridge with inflatable floats revolutionized river crossings for armored units.

British contributions in engine design, aircraft ordnance, and ammunition also boosted American aeronautical progress significantly. Jet aircraft engines, considered feasible by engineers for years, may largely be credited to British pioneering, although the Luftwaffe was the first to employ jet planes operationally despite incredible delays imposed by Hitler's indecision.

Failures Abroad

A review of this decade's military technology, from which the above examples were selected, discovers no nation or group of nations whose record always reflected foresight or even sound common sense. Typical of the myopia of the times were the obsolete design and inadequate numbers of landing craft which the Japanese used in 1941, when, after years of careful planning, they launched one of the greatest amphibious campaigns in history. Japanese troop training had consisted mainly of clambering up and down rope ladders slung from barracks' porches. Overseas transport of troops was a responsibility of the Japanese Army, not Navy, yet the Japanese planners neglected both equipment and training for combat landings.[3]

Germany's logical dependence upon the submarine as the work horse for naval operations was downgraded to permit brilliant, but profitless, efforts in surpassing other navies in the technological superiority of their surface warships. The Kriegsmarine's great strides in improving undersea craft began only after months of war had again demonstrated what should have been the obvious goal of German naval efforts all along.

Nor was Britain wiser in this field of warfare despite her narrow escape from disaster under submarine blockade in 1917. The British gave the undersea threat slight attention in their 1930 research and development. By 1939, her Fleet Air Arm had withered into a neglected component of the Royal Air Force, trying to operate with obsolescent aircraft, few active carriers, and no established tactical doctrine.

[3] Louis Morton, in *Marine Corps Gazette*, April 1956.

By comparison, both Allied and enemy, offensive and defensive, undersea weapons technologies took major jumps under the spur of war, exposing the wholly insufficient development of the 1930s. In this field it could have been written of the Germans, as it was of United States military research, that "most of our difficulties can be traced to a late start."

The United States' lag in jet propulsion was the most serious technical deficiency in American aircraft development during the Second World War. The principle had long been known, but, until the advent of gas turbines in the 1930s, aircraft design was not sufficiently advanced to encourage the development of jet propulsion units. Developments in Germany and Britain began at the same time ('35 and '36). The Air Corps had been aware of jet propulsion potentialities and by 1939 had requested the National Academy of Sciences to study the problem of compression ignition engines in rocket or jet propulsion. Yet, at the war's end both Germany and Britain had operational jets while we had none.

Significantly, the basic discoveries which American scientists and engineers translated into practical use during World War II were almost without exception of European origin. That the dependence of American science on European basic research has not yet been entirely eliminated is a matter of deep concern to those charged with American security. As Vannevar Bush stated: "It is truer than ever that basic research is the pacemaker of technological progress. In the nineteenth century Yankee mechanical ingenuity, building largely upon the basic discoveries of European scientists, could greatly advance the technical arts. Now the situation is different."

Contrasting Concerns

The war-born revolution in America's attitude toward military technology can be demonstrated graphically. In 1950, the armed forces were at work on about 13,000 specific research and development projects; funds for that program amounted to some half-billion dollars. This great level of effort was to be increased manyfold in five short years. The budget for expenditure on research and development (including improved facilities) in the defense services for the fiscal year 1956 was estimated at two billion dollars. Under the pressure of the cold war, these expenditures progressed seventyfold from the $29,000,000 of fiscal year 1940. Some 124,000 persons in the military and civilian departments participated in these programs by 1956. Post-Sputnik emphasis has increased the scope and perhaps the quality of this immense effort.

The Hoover Commission on Organization of the Executive Branch of the Government made this pertinent postwar appraisal: "This organization of research and development in the government is the largest integrated scientific and technical endeavor that any nation has ever attempted. The programs . . . reach through the realm of abstract science, the evolution of scientific discovery into inventions and improvements. In the military departments the development of inventions and improvements in weapons extends into the test of these improvements; the standardization of design; the development of production programs; the placement and co-ordination of production; and, finally, production must be accompanied by continuous further research and constant evaluation of results."[4]

This expansion reflects grave concern over our national security in a period in which technology threatens to become the arbiter of the global conflict. Organized and co-operative military research and development are now a major part of our national overhead. The Federal Government currently exercises the influence and provides the major support for American research and development on a scale beyond the wildest speculation of the military and civilian planners who mobilized our country in World War II.

An equally significant straw in the shifting wind has been the changed attitude of Congress toward our military establishment. This war-generated change can be seen in the following extract from a 1947 House Report:

"It is the belief of the committee that it is highly important that obsolete items of equipment be replaced to the extent necessary to keep the Army trained in the use of the latest type weapons and, at the same time, keep the industry of the country abreast of these developments. This requirement is emphasized in the maintenance of a relatively small, yet completely efficient and modern Air Force. The minimum requirement to achieve this objective during fiscal year 1947, so far as the Air Force is concerned, is estimated to cost $388,776,454 for the procurement of approximately 1046 of the most modern aircraft of all types from very heavy bombers and jet fighters to liaison planes and metal gliders, spare engines and parts, and related air-borne communications' equipment."[5]

[4] "Research and Development in the Government," a Report to the Congress, May 1955, p. xi.

[5] Military Establishment Appropriation Bill, 1947: 80th Congress 2nd Session House of Representatives: Report No. 2311.

These figures already seem ancient history. Since 1947 we have repeatedly seen the unusual spectacle of the Congress urging military expenditures upon the Executive branch. The tight-purse proponents in national defense seem to have shifted their base of operations from the Capitol to the Bureau of the Budget.

During this same decade technological progress has encountered a new roadblock: Service rivalries over strategic roles and missions reflected in bitter struggles to gain exclusive control of new weapons. As one leading scientist, Dr. Lloyd V. Berkner, explained: "Communications have been shut off to serious consideration of any proposal that differs from the current policy of one of the Services."[6]

In the same article, Dr. Berkner commented on the difficulties the military encountered in keeping up with technological advances. He singled out General Omar N. Bradley's valedictory articles that appeared in *The Saturday Evening Post* in 1953, in which the general stated that the aurora borealis made radio and electronic operations uncertain for days at a time, although in demonstration three years earlier inexpensive methods had actually improved communications when the aurora plays.[7]

Technology and Power

Organizational pitfalls not withstanding, technology is now advancing on a broad front. Its new role in the military policy of the United States is the product of two factors: the leadership role which history has thrust upon a

[6] Lloyd V. Berkner, *Bulletin of the Atomic Scientists*, December 1953.
[7] Ibid.

reluctant United States and the belated recognition that national power is now more than ever a measure of technological achievement. Any doubts on this score have been eclipsed by the towering specter of the new "superweapons." We realize that the battle for technological supremacy is now a battle for survival.

For the past several centuries the shift of technical proficiency from country to country has been attended by upheavals in international power, political and military. Where technological change has been swift, notably Germany's two unique surges of development, first at the turn of the century and again under Hitler, international stability was shattered.

Similarly, the technological thrust of Japan produced a series of military and political explosions from 1895 to 1945. The engines of Japanese imperialism were fired by a technology imported wholesale from the West. The mere purchase of arms and equipment would not have lifted Japan from a second-rate power status. National sources of supply had to be firmly established. To provide these sources required indigenous metal production, manufacturing, agriculture, transportation, banking, business administration, governmental organization, and a new system of education.

Today, we face a recurrent challenge in a novel setting. The technologies serving war have vastly expanded. Economists and social scientists have joined the ranks of the physical scientists, themselves only recently drawn into their nation's struggle for security. Armed forces, especially in the United States, do not yet reflect a complete technological response to national defense requirements. Instead, they are still evolving from a complex mixture of inchoate fears, vaguely understood traditions, group interest, and ambitions. For today's military establishment we must devise unprecedented weapons systems "cutting across traditional lines of military organization."[8]

Nor should we count wholly lost to civilian betterment all technological effort devoted to military ends. History records many surprises. François Appert's invention of the tin can for Napoleon's sprawling armies in 1804 started the world's canning industry to preserve foodstuffs. The Chemical Corps' aerosol bomb of World War II grew into a multi-million dollar industry for over three hundred commercial products.

The vast impact of military research on America's domestic economy is just beginning to be known. The prewar dependence of the military on civilian technology has been reversed. Now many civilian products and techniques are the direct result of military needs which inspired R&D programs. Contributions of military R&D to civilian life which are well known include: "yellow-fever eradication, chlorination of water, nuclear power, blood-plasma substitutes, the modern aircraft, new high-temperature alloys, and the modern automobile automatic transmission system. Other contributions not so well known, though none the less valuable, include nitrogen-mustard treatment of leukemia and other cancers, many of the better insecticides and rodenticides, mechanical smoke generators for crop protection, flameproof fabrics, heat-resistant and fire-retarding paints, aircraft engines, helicopters, anti-icing equipment, new plastics and adhesives, new automobile power-steering and suspension systems, advanced weather-prediction techniques, tissue-bank techniques, miniature electronic components, auto-

[8] Lloyd V. Berkner, *Bulletin of the Atomic Scientists*, December 1953.

mation, silicon transistors, and automatic electronic computers."[9]

The path followed from "a military need" to a new civilian product of great importance is most instructive. "Not only does it indicate the close relationship between military R&D and the civilian economy, but also the role of government where only large sums of money, usually not willingly 'gambled' by private industry in the absence of the prospect of a short-run pay-off, bring about innovations much earlier than might normally be the case."[10]

President Eisenhower has given impetus to the incalculable potential of the "atoms for peace" program which originated in the war-born Manhattan Report. In such endeavors unstinted attention to science and engineering is only a start. We also require "research into forces devolving upon people who must make decisions . . . how to develop our military strength, when and where to apply it, how to ensure that it furthers, not hinders, our political ends."[11]

Obsolescence and Lead Time

The new predominance of technology as a determinant of national power carries with it some built-in restraints and complications. On the one hand, there has been a vast multiplication of new ideas in weaponry. Discovery seems to beget discovery, and the rate of proliferation is constantly accelerat-

[9] Operations Research Office, the Johns Hopkins University: *Defense Spending and the U. S. Economy*, Vol. I, June 1958, p. 17.

[10] Ibid.

[11] W. T. R. Fox, Preface to Bibliography of *Civil-Military Relations*, Social Science Research Council, 1954.

ing. The decision-making burdens on the men who must constantly choose among perplexing alternatives, e.g., missiles or bombers, hardening or mobility, what type shelters for civil defense, are ever more staggering. At the same time, weapons themselves become more and more complex. Eighty times as many engineering man hours went into producing fighter aircraft in 1955 as in 1940. Weaponry's lead time, from concept to finished operation, grows longer yearly. The life span of each new weapon constantly shrinks. Today, many weapons are already stamped by obsolescence by the time they become available in quantity for operational use; the B-36 long-range bomber or the first Nike anti-aircraft missile are typical examples.

This rapid obsolescence emphasizes the vital importance of peacetime research and development. Since national security now relies heavily upon technical proficiency of personnel, peacetime military strategic planning must be supported by a vigorous program of scientific research and development, buttressed by intensive technical training. At the current rate of weapons mortality, there will be no time to complete "Manhattan Projects" in a future war. The tools of victory in such a struggle will have been forged in the laboratories of the victor five to fifteen years before the start of hostilities.

Increasing official recognition of this fact is attested to by a Congressional report: "The importance of peacetime research and development cannot be too highly stressed. Even under the most favorable conditions there is a long period of time between the conception of the need for an item of equipment and its development, test, production, and eventual delivery to the services. Our success or failure in the initial stages of an emergency could, therefore, very well depend largely upon the adequacy of our peacetime research and development. In any future emergency the initial stages may be critical, since we may be forced to engage in active operations before our military potential could be mobilized."[12]

Stiffer Training

Technology is also placing a heavy demand upon the Armed Forces to recruit and train a new kind of fighting man. It has immensely expanded the need for large cadres of highly skilled technicians in the Armed Forces. Military manpower tables reflect this revolution in manpower requirements. Typical modern servicemen are the guided missileman and aviation fire-control technician in the Navy, each of whom requires a training period of about 25 months. The following historical contrast of percentages of scientific and technical manpower in the Navy indicates the new trend:[13]

Period	Technical manpower % of all ratings
Civil War	2.8
Spanish-American War	2.9
World War I	2.5
World War II	6.4
Korean Conflict	10.8
1954	13.4

[12] National Military Establishment Appropriation Bill, 1950, 81st Congress: 1st Session, House of Representatives: Report No. 417.

[13] "Science, Technology and Manpower," Rear Admiral Rawson Bennett, Journal of the American Society of Naval Engineers, Inc., February 1956.

Despite our most energetic efforts, technology threatens to outrace the growing force of men trained to tame it. Already, the armed forces are staggering under the complexity of scientific expansion. The increasing application of science and technology to warfare has brought about the integration of the operating elements into "weapons systems." Single elements of a given system cannot be developed independently of others. The "system's" technical and manpower requirements and those of each of its elements must be established through a continuing "give and take" between the elements.

Once a highly developed weapons system has been devised, we can no longer think in terms of the weapon alone, or the man alone. New weapons create new personnel problems. For this reason the study of man himself has become an essential part of our research and development program. The military are constantly turning to such fields as medicine, psychology,[14] and the social sciences. In these, as well as in the various branches of technology, the Armed Forces must keep abreast of progress and change. The elaborate process whereby the nation selected and began training its first astronauts dramatically epitomizes this trend.

A related effort is the study of weapon and equipment design, the specific aim being to increase their ease and convenience of operation. A high degree of co-ordination is needed to operate many weapons. If weapon controls are too complicated, the soldier's job will be needlessly difficult. Human engineering, which plays a vital part in modern

[14] During the Korean conflict, successful cures (soldiers returning to combat duties) of neuropsychiatric disorders (once vaguely referred to as "shell shock") more than trebled the rate experienced in World War II.

industrial design, is indispensable in producing the most effective man-weapon system. The adaptation of the interior design of our nuclear submarines to human limitations is but one case in point.

When superior weapons are combined with capable soldiers, we have the main ingredients of effective military forces. Calculating the most efficient and economical ways of using the two ingredients in military operations, i.e., tactical problems in the nuclear age, has brought scientists into yet another area of military development. It is now almost as common for civilian scientists to be consulted in operational matters in which men are joined with machines as in the design and building of complex weapons.

The need for technically trained military manpower is growing. We need far more individuals who can adapt for military use the bold new weapons which new technology is building, as well as the scientists and engineers who create them.

The Challenge Ahead

Through participation in World War II, the United States left an era when it could safely neglect military technology and entered a period in which technology is the staple of survival. Technology, as has been observed, changes most rapidly of all the major elements of national power. The uncomfortable fact we must face is that the speed with which these changes occur, already high by World War II, is constantly accelerating. Under these circumstances, complacency, fostered by success in the recent past, could spell disaster.

With remarkable foresight, William James once wrote, "Every up-to-date dictionary should say that peace and war mean the same thing now *in posse*, now *in actu*. It may even be reasonably said that intensely sharp competitive preparation for war by the nation is the real war, permanent, unceasing; and that battles are only a sort of public verification of mastery gained during the peace intervals."[15]

The future of the United States so starkly hinges on the outcome of this struggle for mastery in which we now find ourselves.

[15] *Memories and Studies*, William James, p. 273.

CHAPTER VII

TECHNOLOGY AND NATIONAL SURVIVAL

TO AMERICANS IT SEEMED UNTHINKABLE, AT THE END OF World War II, that the United States could ever lose the industrial and technological superiority it displayed in winning that global conflict. America's main technological competitor, Germany, had been liquidated. Great Britain, our principal ally, the other most advanced industrial nation of the Western world, was too impoverished to keep up with the U.S. potential in military technology. Russia was generally regarded as years behind the Western world in all phases of industrial progress and in most fields of science. The United States, it was believed, could easily keep ahead of the Soviet Union technologically.

The mark of our times was the rapidity with which this belief was to die. In the fall of 1957, the Soviets celebrated the fortieth anniversary of the Bolshevik Revolution with a boastful exhibit of the weaponry which marked the transformation, within four decades, of earthbound peasants into front-runners in the battle for space. On the very day the Russians paraded their military might in Red Square, Americans listened to President Eisenhower's assessment of our military posture. The President admitted that the United States military development program was lagging and pledged action. He spoke some reassuring words: "As of today, the over-all military strength of the free world is distinctly greater than that of Communist countries. . . ." Nevertheless, the President warned, "It is entirely possible that in the years ahead we could fall behind."

How did the West, particularly the United States, lose so much of its technological lead in so short a time?

Quantity Versus Quality

It may be that our massive technological achievements in World War II tended to blind us to the fact that they had been outstanding more in quantity than in quality. Unheeded were the complaints of armored fighters who pointed to the inferiority of their matériel compared with Germany's powerful Tiger tanks, the British special-purpose armor and the austere combat efficiency of the Stalin tank series. Rocketry had been pioneered in America, but the "V" weapons launched against England had been developed by Nazi technology.

The significant contribution of radar to victory in a series of decisive battles owed more to British than to American research and development. Even the United States debt to foreign science in the success of the Manhattan (atomic bomb) Project was scarcely noted outside scientific circles.

Such faint discordant notes had been ignored in the atmosphere of "total victory." The endless stream of American equipment and munitions, once the tide of production reached flood heights, had amazed our allies and doomed our foes. We rested on our laurels and relaxed our effort to continue the military exploitation of science.

This complacency was compounded by our myopic view of the military situation. United States military policy in 1946 was based on possession of the atomic bomb, a monopoly which we expected to retain for years. Overconfident, we even slighted the long-range development of aircraft essential to deliver, should the need arise, our "ultimate weapon."

Postwar demobilization decisively weakened America's military power developed through four years of struggle and sacrifice. While the dismantling process was relatively less drastic than after previous wars (we still maintained a modest research and development program), the nascent alliance between the scientific community and the military was weakened by discord and indifference. Scientists sought a greater voice in the choice of military projects and their manner of development. This pressure was reflected in the creation of the civilian Atomic Energy Commission to replace the Army's Manhattan Project. All these factors—the desire to turn again to peaceful pursuits, the strained relations between soldiers and scientists, the sharp decrease in appropriations—produced a hiatus in the imaginative, long-range development of weapons.

Efforts to close this gap were sporadic and abortive until the outbreak of the Korean War, although the West had awakened much earlier to the extent of Soviet ambitions. The warning had been sounded by Winston Churchill in his "Iron Curtain" speech at Fulton, Missouri, in the spring of 1946. Nevertheless, the initial programs developed by our government to meet the Soviet threat were, on the whole, nonmilitary in character and implemented by economic means. The Marshall Plan was one such program; the decision to back Greece and Turkey was another. In a sense, we countered Communist expansion chiefly with dollars, without providing either a political basis or a military underpinning for our economic diplomacy. Vaguely, we relied upon our atomic monopoly as though it were both permanent and omnipotent, even while we furiously debated the "morality" of ever using it.

The Soviet Bid

Stalin announced Soviet long-range policy in a celebrated speech at the Kremlin on February 9, 1946. In this speech, he invoked all of the old Communist shibboleths of "Western imperialism." He reverted to orthodox Communist tenets and attributed the recent global war to conflict among the capitalist powers over markets.

Stalin openly termed Russia's wartime alliance with the Western democracies a transitory expedient, warning that the Soviet Union must prepare defenses against the inevitable attack of predatory capitalism upon the homeland of socialism. Simultaneously, he announced a dramatic build-up of Soviet military power. This build-up was, in fact, merely a continuation of the long-range program of industrial and technological development which the first Five Year Plan had launched in 1928. Stalin's 1946 speech made it clear that the Soviets intended to return to that war-interrupted program with renewed vigor.

To the Communists, technology and military arms are instruments for the seizure and expansion of political power.

Creative scientists within the Soviet Union have always been awarded a privileged position in the hierarchy of Communist "classless" society; even in the great purge of 1937, distinguished members of this group fared better than their colleagues in other fields. We are just now beginning to understand the bearing of the Soviet educational system upon the growth of Soviet technology. Scientific manpower is only a rough indicator and not a fully reliable index of scientific potential; yet, the Soviet technological training program gives us no cause for complacency. According to reliable reports, Russia, in 1955, graduated at least twice as many engineers as the United States. During his visit to the United States in 1959 Khrushchev boasted that the Soviet Union has raised the ratio in its favor to three to one.

Nor should we minimize the quality of Soviet technology. Russian scientific aptitude has long been evident; today, with increased and better training facilities being made available both at the college and postgraduate levels, their potential for developing exceptional scientists is increased. In all, the U.S.S.R. is building a technological labor force, qualified in every respect, which may draw abreast of that of the United States early in the 1960s.

These strides have not been wholly the result of indigenous efforts. At the close of World War II, the Soviet Union still lacked the requisite scientists and engineers for Stalin's military policy. Consequently, in 1945, the Soviet Union intensified the importation of the latest scientific and technical know-how. This campaign took many forms. Part of it was the seizure and enticement of German scientists. They were given the necessary facilities to continue in the Soviet Union the projects which they had begun under Hitler. The Soviet Union also conducted a systematic exploitation of the readily available scientific literature of the free world. To obtain information not so readily available, an extensive espionage campaign, concentrated in the atomic energy field, probed the military and technological secrets of the United States, Canada, Great Britain, and other Western countries. The record shows that the general trend of the work of the Manhattan Project, so secret to most Americans, was known by Soviet Intelligence as early as 1943.

These co-ordinated efforts paid off. The first Soviet atomic bomb, exploded in 1949, preceded by at least three years the date predicted by the most knowledgeable officials in the American atomic energy field. Since then, Soviet progress has been equally startling in almost every field of military technology.

A brief review of Soviet methods and achievements may be useful. The German invasion of Russia retarded the technological revolution, initiated by Stalin. Most of the arms and aircraft factories in western Russia were destroyed, but the U.S.S.R. was able to transfer enough machinery to re-establish plants east of the Urals. Although American Lend-Lease shipments contributed to Soviet victories, the U.S.S.R. probably produced at least 85 per cent of all its military requirements during the war. Whatever the combination of Russian efforts and Allied contributions, the Soviets recouped early losses to achieve, before the end of the war, a quantitative and, in some cases, qualitative military-technological superiority over their German foe.

The advent of peace accelerated the Soviet drive for military power based on a high level of technological proficiency. A primary objective of Soviet policy, following World War II, was to achieve technological-industrial parity with, and

215

eventually superiority over, the United States. This objective has been pursued relentlessly under centralized direction.

America's atomic monopoly and long-range bomber capabilities forced the Kremlin to concentrate initially upon weapons of defense, even while Soviet atomic weapons and long-range air offense were being developed. At the outbreak of the Korean War this first objective had been achieved in terms of the technological levels of 1950; hundreds of advanced MIG fighter aircraft were pitted in Korea against a more limited number of American bombers and fighter planes. Progress in Soviet offensive capabilities can be measured by America's slender lead in the race for the hydrogen bomb, the development of high-performance heavy bombers and, most disturbing, of all, startling Soviet successes in missile weaponry.

The Soviet Union was the first to recognize the military potentials of Nazi-inaugurated missile weapons. Crash programs were instituted in the various missile fields, without weakening the Red Army's position as the world's predominant land force or slowing the pace of Soviet Air Force expansion.

Real Soviet security expenditures have increased since 1957—at steadily rising rates. Far from declining as a percentage of the budget the real military outlays seem to be increasing in terms of both. Also the invisible side of the 1960 Soviet security budget appears to be about as large as its visible side.

Half of the Soviet security outlay is hidden in other budget items; some expenditures are even outside the budget. Every year the budget mentions "expenditures for scientific research," financed chiefly out of the social and cultural budget and secondarily out of "organizational" funds. These outlays have risen fourfold between 1951 and 1960. Whenever fulfillment figures were given, they show overspending. The 1960 plan provided for research some 15 per cent more than was spent in 1959, some 19 per cent more than planned for 1959.

In reality, Soviet research expenditures are even higher than the amount publicized. Additional sums are obtained, for instance, from the "national economy" budget. On the other hand, it must be noted that not all expenditures for scientific research are of a military nature; the category refers to all kinds of research.

The Soviet military outlay may represent 12–13 per cent of the 1960 gross national product. The U.S. devotes to national security about 9 per cent of a GNP that is more than twice as large as the Soviet. But because Soviet armed forces personnel are poorly paid and the armament industry is the most efficient sector of the Soviet economy, the U.S.S.R. is able with much smaller resources to obtain a larger package of military goods and services than the United States. Valuing Soviet weapons and manpower at dollar prices, the military effort of the U.S.S.R. was about equal to that of the United States in 1959. In the early 1960s a gap in favor of the U.S.S.R. could develop.

Instead of sponsoring major efforts to improve the lot of the Russian people, the Soviet leaders chose a ruthless policy of advancing military and technological power to the exclusion of almost any other consideration. All areas of technology associated with military strength, including the steel industry, electrical power, machine tools, automation, aluminum, propulsion systems of all kinds, were greatly expanded and improved in a single decade.

In short, military requirements were given top priority in

the Soviet economy—a condition which contrasts starkly with the proportionately small American economic effort which goes into the technology of military production. Since the end of the war, the Soviet Union has maintained its ready forces at a higher degree of combat preparedness than ever before. The United States, pursuing a defensive strategy, should logically maintain forces significantly superior to those of the U.S.S.R. rather than being content with parity. That we have not done so is a matter of increasing concern.

Technological Comparison

Where do we stand today relative to the Soviet Union in the technological race? Whatever the exact answer, it is probable that, during the next five to ten years, the Communist empire will achieve, in some key areas, technological equality with the United States and, in selected fields, technological superiority. The record supports such a forecast. Indeed, in some areas the Soviets may already have forged ahead of the United States.

Whenever the Soviet Union has concentrated its effort, complicated weapon systems have been produced in remarkably short times. In a few but critical fields, these weapons tend to surpass our own. The crucial danger confronting the United States is our continued reliance on qualitative superiority and its corollary: failure to provide adequate, ready military formations in all categories.

Because the West concedes the initiative, moreover, the Soviet leaders enjoy far greater freedom of technological action. We must be prepared to meet any thrust the Kremlin may make in any sphere or with any type of weapons system. Committed by our own policy to remain on the defensive, we must disperse our strength while our opponent can efficiently concentrate his resources in support of his secretly chosen strategy.

The Soviets, even before they were known to have attained any qualitative superiority, had outproduced the United States in military hardware by allocating a greater proportion of their resources to that purpose. Equally significant has been their ability to reduce the lead time required to produce major items of equipment. In the U.S.S.R., for comparable types of aircraft, the period from drawing board through mock-up to operational prototype has been one half of that consumed in this country. Soviet decision-making procedures and techniques for integrating components into a production model have proved extremely effective.

There is no reason to recount here Soviet advances in nuclear weapons, missile design, electronic equipment—their success in such matters as radar and electronic warfare measures. Nor has this remarkable progress interfered with unparalleled strides in mechanizing a large army and developing a major naval arm to displace Great Britain from second rank in world sea power. They have concentrated especially upon their submarine force, presently three times that possessed by Germany at the height of World War II and approximately four times the U. S. Navy's announced strength in underwater craft.

The U.S.S.R. still commits almost half its labor to agriculture, compared to 10 per cent for the United States. Yet, Moscow plows back one-fifth of total Russian resources, year after year, into investment—a figure we attain only when our economy, much of it devoted to supercomfort, reaches very high levels. The divergence is even greater in investment allocation. Half the Soviet investment is in industry as against one-fourth of ours, 15 per cent for housing in contrast with 25 per cent for the U.S., 9 per cent for "miscellaneous"—largely "luxury" items—compared to 30 per cent for this country. Thus, technological and scientific expansion is carried on ruthlessly at the expense of basic population comforts.[1]

The United States, having belatedly realized its deficiencies, is making a concerted effort in research and development in the field of military technology. Again, however, in relative terms, this effort is small in relation to our gross national product. It appears still smaller when compared with Soviet allocations to military technological projects. In summary, the Soviet Union has become a worthy competitor of the United States in many realms of general technology and threatens to surpass us in technology applied to military needs.

Why does the United States permit the Soviet Union to outstrip it in a contest for technological superiority? In truth, most Americans still discount the possibility that the Soviets might win such a race. Even the furor caused by the Sputniks has largely subsided. Statements in the press by Americans in many fields cast doubt on the grim fact that we are running a technological race for survival. Increasingly lulled by a luxurious living standard and comfortably secure in the belief that the American genius will somehow make up for our past shortcomings, we content ourselves with an inadequate defense program.

Thus, we hopefully concentrate our military technology

[1] J. A. Kershaw, *Statistics from American Academy of Political Sciences,* January 1959.

upon improving a long-range striking force, whether aircraft or missiles, to deter general war. Yet, the requirements which might deter, or win, limited war are neglected. For example, Mark S. Watson reported a "thrilling demonstration [at Aberdeen Proving Ground] of a new gun-stabilizer in the Patton tank." This successful test model followed by some dozen years the operationl azimuth and elevation stabilizers in Nazi Tiger tanks used against our armor in World War II. The delay in acquiring comparable devices, according to Watson, was due to the "crippling economy [in ground force weapons] starting before V-J Day and continuing to the Korean conflict." At that time, a crash basis rearmament program froze existing models. The sizable Army matériel build-up of 1950–53 is obsolete today and plans to modernize the Army have been placed low down in Defense Department priorities.[2] Obsessed with the belief that general war means a one-day holocaust, we concentrate our sparse defensive efforts on measures which will insure the launching of our retaliatory force before it is destroyed.

Inflexible tactics are as risky in the military laboratory as they are on the battlefield. Unstinted efforts to improve our deterrent power must rate top priority in our overall military program, but they should not constitute the entire program. Technological superiority in weapons systems for limited war is an essential antidote for the slow but deadly poison of creeping aggression. Finally, we cannot ignore the vital area of defense: the technological miracles of this century serve ample notice that a defense breakthrough, dismissed as fantasy by many authorities, could, if achieved, upset the nuclear stalemate as abruptly as one in offensive weapons.

[2] *Ordnance* magazine, February 1957.

The Rockefeller Report: Four Factors

There has been a disturbing tendency, both in and out of government, to blink at unpleasant truths. A notable exception was the Rockefeller Brothers Fund report *International Security—The Military Aspect*.[3] This review of United States security included the following assessment of our technological performance:

"It is our judgment, that all is not well with present U.S. security policies and operations. The over-all U.S. strategic concept lags behind developments in technology and in the world political situation. In major respects defense organization is unrelated to critically important military missions. Systems of budgets, appropriations, and financial management are out of gear with the radically accelerating flow of military developments. The U.S. is rapidly losing its lead in the race of military technology. . . .

". . . Four factors—the importance of a growing industrial base, the crucial role of lead times, the increasing significance of forces-in-being, and the necessity of a versatile military establishment—impose on policy makers an unparalleled problem of choice. It is further complicated by the explosive rapidity with which technology is developing. . . . Moreover . . . each new weapons system costs more than double its predecessor which it replaces at shorter and shorter intervals.

"This technological race places an extraordinary premium

[3] *International Security: The Military Aspect.* Copyright © 1958 by Rockefeller Brothers Fund, Inc. Reprinted by permission of Doubleday & Company, Inc.

on the ability to assess developing trends correctly, to make and back decisions firmly and to be prepared to change plans when necessary. It also places the side which is on the defensive at special disadvantage . . . [to] gear its planning and procurement to the possibility of an attack at any moment."

Finally, to overcome some of the conspicuous weaknesses noted in our security system, the report concludes: "The above deficiencies in our strategic posture can be removed only by substantially increased defense expenditures. These increases will run into billions of dollars and must rise substantially in each of the next few years."

The United States possesses the total resources to stay on top technologically. Unquestionably, the American people, once properly impressed with the need, will back their leaders in implementing such an effort. The question boils down to an understanding of the gravity of the problem and the determination to find the answers, whatever the cost in dollars, devotion, and sacrifice. The history of our "too little and too late" preparations for every war we have fought since the 1890s should caution us against believing that this turn of affairs will come about automatically. Democracies have always been perilously shortsighted in their approach to the problem of their own survival.

There are a number of logical ways in which our leaders can assure the United States of qualitative superiority in weapons systems. First, we must allot sufficient resources, in both money and manpower, to technological progress. There is a tendency to cede strong influence on technical decisions to "budgeteers." The men in charge of the budget are prone, as a matter of course, to concentrate funds on "sure things" at the neglect of promising "risk projects."

This predilection, together with the perennial debate in Congress over the national budget, has resulted in serious fluctuations in the amount of money allocated to vital development programs. Intermittent support of research projects wastes time and scientific effort as well as dollars.

We must make available more systematic training in technology for military personnel so that our military strategy can be fashioned by knowledgeable military planners—in cooperation with the men in the laboratories and behind the drawing boards. A step in this direction would be to place more emphasis on technology in the curriculums of the major war colleges which train the future commanders of our military establishment. Likewise, greater stress should be placed on advanced study in science and technology for selected officers during the early years of their military service. Finally, career noncommissioned officers and enlisted technicians must be developed by suitable means to reduce the inefficiencies of short term of service soldiers.

We must also make an attempt to solve the problem of recruiting and training the highly qualified scientific and engineering manpower essential to maintain simultaneously an expanding civilian economy and win the arms race. To this end, we need more elaborate scientific research centers of the highest caliber.

Even in terms of applied technology, the supply of scientists and engineers in the United States has not kept pace with the ever growing demand. Nor have the material rewards for applied science been such as to draw enough men of genius into "pure" science. Our present methods of selecting students for higher scientific education and their subsequent training and management no longer fill the strident needs of the day. Many of our key research and development projects are braked by shortages in human rather than material resources. The United States government's responsibilities for promoting scientific research and development require the means and incentives for training scientists and engineers sufficient to our needs. Finally, better management of our technological programs must cut down decision-lead times on choices and streamline procedures for administering technological development.

Technology in the Affluent Society

True, the problems which confront us are formidable. For example, as the number of available design choices grow with incredible rapidity, who is wholly qualified to select new weapons? How can we best integrate the tactics and logistics of military men with the diverse skills of scientists, engineers, and civilian cabinet members? Are our decision makers as aware of "costs" in terms of time as they are budget conscious? What is their understanding of weapons systems, not merely weapons?

The Soviet technological advance has proceeded at a faster rate than that of the West for several fundamental reasons:

"First is a continuous sense of awareness and decision, both by planners and those who carry out plans, as to the direction and relative priority of projects. Second, with these fairly clear objectives in mind, the Soviet decision making structure itself is more responsive and immediate in its reactions. Third, once decisions and priorities are established, efforts are devoted to a particular project in proportion to its priority, almost regardless of cost.

The result is that Soviet lead time for complex weapons

systems development and other technical projects tends to be shorter than our own. This reduced lead time stems not from greater intellectual or technical capacity, but from the will to take and make decisions and then to produce results. The Soviets decide to finish a project at a certain point in time. We decide either to finish a project that costs X dollars, or to finish it on a later date because we have only X-Y dollars. The crucial factor, however, is really the target date for making the device operational. The Soviets allocate funds according to strategic priorities, but do not determine priorities or strategies according to available funds."[4]

Another serious problem lies in the mounting expense inherent even in the most carefully drawn system of priorities. If we rely upon the growth of our gross national product to permit greater allocations to military technology without drawing upon the luxuries in the civilian side of our economy, the record of the last five years disappoints us. A hope that more efficient direction of our defense establishment, particularly its research, development and procurement aspects, will bring higher returns per dollar despite inflationary pressures, suggests marginal gains at best.

Eminent economists deny that current allocations to defense, approximately 10 per cent of our gross national product, cannot be safely raised 50 per cent or more. The Committee for Economic Development, composed of top-flight businessmen, industrialists, and financiers, with its own competent research staff, had this to say on this thorny issue:

"Fear that a high defense burden will weaken the economy has been exaggerated and should not be decisive in

[4] Curriculum, National Strategy Seminar for Reserve Officers, The National War College, prepared by Foreign Policy Research Institute, University of Pennsylvania, July 1959, p. 33.

the determination of the size of a defense budget representing 10 to 15 per cent of the gross national product, or even more. There is no factual basis for the notion that we are within reach or exceeding some 'breaking point' beyond which tax-financed expenditures will critically impair economic growth . . . *We can afford what we have to afford.*"[5]

The basic question remains for solution, as it has throughout our history, in the conscience of the American people. Do we intend to gamble our freedom on the belief that Soviet intentions are and will remain peaceful? Has our urge for ever greater luxuries become so insistent that our security requirements can be swept aside by consumer demand in the world's most "affluent society"? Politicians shun the prospect of requisite tax increases. Statesmen may well pose the choice of our children's future versus second cars and color television. Communized people have, per force, already substituted "guns for butter."

The problems of allocating sufficient effort to the technological and industrial aspects of military security are discussed in *The Affluent Society*[6] by John K. Galbraith. As he stated, "if a high standard of living is central in the American way of life, it will even be said that it is paradoxical to abandon it in a war to preserve the American way of life. With time and effort the paradox can perhaps be resolved, but for that the leaders must have the requisite understanding."

Galbraith advanced this point succinctly when he stated that in World War II "our presumed civilian needs kept

[5] *The Problem of National Security,* July 1958, page 52. Prepared by the Research and Policy Committee of the Committee for Economic Development.

[6] Houghton Mifflin Company, 1958, p. 172.

millions of men from facing the enemy or from supporting with weapons and supplies those that did." Had we lost the war we would have learned that lesson. In developing this thesis he alluded to the R.A.F. attacks on Hamburg in which firestorms killed more people than were killed at Hiroshima. Living areas were completely gutted, but the peripheral factories were unhurt. Galbraith suggested that this actually increased the military effectiveness of the Germans by reducing "drastically consumption of unessentials and employment of men in their supply." This line of argument can, of course, be carried to extremes. It does point out, however, that the "direct correlation between national power and economic output" which has become "imbedded in conventional wisdom as the new dimension of military power" has little relation to reality. In short, the adequacy of peacetime preparations for a possible conflict do not depend on the size of the economy but how much can or will be diverted for defense preparations. The implications to the United States are obvious. Our wealth is a valuable asset but as things stand now it is largely unavailable since we do not make proper use of our affluence for the fundamental purposes of survival. Perhaps until we change our economic attitudes in which luxuries are regarded as necessities this failure will persist.

The failure to make optimum use of the great industrial capacity of the United States in the conflict with the Communist bloc could have disastrous consequences. These were underscored by Richard Foster's comparison of the relative advantages in the power balance. According to Foster,[7] the Soviet Union appeared to have an advantage in five factors,

[7] S.R.I. *Journal*, Stanford Research Institute, Fourth Quarter, 1959, Vol. III, "Values, Power, and Strategy," pp. 192–93.

i.e., geopolitical, relative population density, the organization of government, will, and intelligence access. In the face of the real advantages of the Soviet Union the United States had two extremely important and, Foster hoped, decisive advantages on its side for the next decade: the American economy, flexible, expansible to extents not yet tested, and on national values—freedom and dignity of the individual. Foster contended that the use we made of them will be a test of our national resolution and the depth of our faith in our convictions.

Once we decide to enter this struggle with greater intensity we should not, however, attempt to "go it alone" in the crucial competition with communism. Our NATO allies and Japan possess industrial resources and pools of skilled scientists and engineers which we cannot afford to neglect. In Sir Winston Churchill's words: "Technological progress is of vast significance to our Commonwealth and to the United States. It is a theme on which the English-speaking peoples can and must work in concert, disregarding national boundaries and seeking unity in the benefits their joint efforts can offer to all men."

Despite the desirablity of such scientific co-operation a NATO-wide effort to mobilize the technological resources of its members is just getting under way.

"Until less than two years ago, rigid security regulations, inherited from our World War II security practices, to a large degree prevented sufficient disclosure of our advances to permit efficient co-operative utilization of European scientific capabilities—a partial exception being the United Kingdom. This policy was changed late in 1957 to permit increased exchange of classified technical defense information.

"Our country's principal effort to stimulate European weapons developments had begun in the fall of 1953 with the establishment of the program now known as the Mutual Weapons Development Program (MWDP). Its purpose was to provide United States financial, and, to the extent possible, technical assistance to highly promising weapons development projects of our North Atlantic Treaty allies, and other friendly nations. The program was soon broadened to include support of technical centers needed by our North Atlantic Treaty military commands."[8]

Qualified scientists and technologists, here and overseas, can contribute only through organized laboratories backed by adequate resources. Their efforts will also require a greater co-ordination between the military and political leaders who direct our military-technological programs. Strategic and tactical concepts cannot be put together haphazardly after each is developed along separate paths. There may be, for instance, a basic incompatability between a policy of "collective security" and a strategy largely dependent upon ICBMs. The logic of the impact of a dynamic technological revolution calls for the assumption by our government, of the degree of leadership which it displayed in the years 1942–45. Unless we improve our machinery for dealing with military technology and find ways and means to give it greater support, there is grave danger that we will slip farther behind, year by year, in a contest we yet refuse to acknowledge.

[8] Composite Report of the President's Committee to Study the United States Military Assistance Program, ("Draper Committee") Volume I (August 17, 1959), p. 159.

Technology: Servant or Master

Our study of the influence of technology on American military policy has traced that influence for some sixty years. Throughout most of that period technology's impact upon our national defense policies was insignificant. Today technological considerations approach dominance in policy determination.

We are living in the midst of a technological revolution. The impact of recent tremendous advances challenges our habitual ways of thinking about national and foreign policy. In the past, military conflicts were fought by soldiers in the front lines; today, the entire population of a nation, is, in a sense, engaged in producing and maintaining the means with which a relatively small corps of experts carries on the actual combat. At the same time, that population is exposed to risks much graver than those which confronted the soldiers on the battlefields of Flanders and Verdun.

In the past, nations mobilized their strength, manpower, industry, transportation networks, material resources to meet the challenge of war. Blitzkriegs menaced only relatively small countries adjacent to a militarized neighbor. Today's technologies have made close neighbors of all nations while cutting available mobilization time from months to hours.

The driving impetus of Soviet technology and the military forces which it supports is calculated to advance the power of the Soviet Union. Technology, in short, is but one pillar in an all-embracing structure of industrial force, weapons and techniques comprising the Communist conflict strategy. This strategy, called Protracted Conflict,[9] prescribes a strategy for annihilating the opponent by more or less limited operations, by feints and maneuvers, psychological manipulation, and various forms of violence. Technology is only one, albeit a very important, segment of the total spectrum of conflict. In the past we allowed our weapons technology to lag. We are now drifting toward the dangerous pitfall of permitting technology to dominate our strategic thinking. What we need is a conceptual grasp of the role of technology within the total range of our security problems so scientific advances can be tailored to our national purposes.

In this context we can see how pernicious is the belief that, once we catch up with or surpass the Soviets in missile technology, most of our problems in meeting the many-pronged Communist challenge will be solved. Despite the over-all technological and industrial superiority we have until recently enjoyed, the Kremlin's masters of political warfare, subversion and infiltration have scored repeated victories. True, we must move faster in the race for technological supremacy or forfeit the struggle. But we must also sharpen our skills and finesse in the nonmilitary areas of conflict.

Summation

As one looks back over the past sixty years he sees a vast panorama in which the United States, growing ever more powerful, only sporadically appreciated the responsibility to the world community devolving upon the possessor of such power. Throughout the first six decades of this century we

[9] For a succinct description of this total strategy see *Protracted Conflict*, Robert Strausz-Hupé and others, Harper & Brothers, 1959.

have repeatedly shown lack of an intelligent appreciation of the role of military establishments as a firm base of national policy and a successful foreign policy. Having no desire to disturb the favorable, to us, *status quo* among nations and forgetting our frequent resort to conflict, we temporarily sought between world wars an impossible security and isolation.

We have abandoned isolationism without fully grasping the fundamentals of how America's security is affected by the technology of the nuclear age.

"The military position of the United States has declined in the short span of 15 years from one of unchallenged security to that of a nation both open and vulnerable to direct and devastating attack. This decline coincides with the rising military power of the Soviet Union, but the Soviet challenge could not have been made with such swiftness and success were it not for developments in military technology enabling that nation to threaten the security of the continental United States.

The most significant of these postwar innovations in military technology can be usefully regarded as a sequence of weapons generations—the conventional, the nuclear, and the nuclear-missile generations. Each has had a distinct and important impact on the strategic equation and the policies of both adversaries; their cumulative effect, however, has been to deprive this Nation of an unquestionably secure military position that was based on its geographic location and a comparatively advanced technology."[10]

[10] *Developments in Military Technology and Their Impact on United States Strategy and Foreign Policy;* A Study prepared at the request of the Committee on Foreign Relations, United States Senate, by the Washington Center of Foreign Policy Research, The Johns Hopkins University, Washington: Government Printing Office, 1959, p. 3.

In short-lived fright we have made proper acknowledgments to disturbing facts emblazoned in the skies but we continue to act, almost as we have always acted, from the pragmatic point of view of a nation of operators.

For this reason today's crying need for long-range technological planning is somehow ignored. Always, prior to the nuclear age, accidents of geography, national resources, and the status of other world powers permitted us to meet emergencies after they confronted us and to surmount them by belated although Herculean efforts.

The new technology, unlike the old, is no longer our perennial ally. Geography has lost much of its earlier significance. The scientific race is at breakneck gallop but construction lead times have lengthened interminably. Warning time in which to guard against a hostile blow has been forfeited. These technical changes challenge the United States far more vitally than the passing of our two-and-a-half-century frontier. They have thrust themselves upon us in a single life span; their cumulating survive-or-perish threat has become apparent only in the last decade.

The accidents of history favored America's initial growth. We have remarked on the fortuitous arrival of the Industrial Revolution which simultaneously enabled us to carry out the conquest of the American wilderness and at the same time to engross the energies of Europe so that we were free from external interference. But the nuclear age of technological upheaval has, on the contrary, operated against this country. It has coincided with the climactic rise of a system dedicated to the destruction of the *status quo* which we find so much in our favor. We ignore the fact that the Communists are Marxists. They are economic determinists who fundamentally believe that technology in the long run will determine the earth's political order. Under these circumstances, to fail to cope with the technological challenge posed by the Soviet Union could lead to our total undoing.

Index

Index